THE GIFT OF GIVING

MUZAHID KHAN

THE GIFT OF GIVING

Dedications

The Prophet Muhammad (PBUH) said: "Even a smile is charity."

First Published in the UK 2020
Swan Signatures paperback edition 2022.

Published by Vellum Publishing,
Turing House, 5 Archway, Manchester M15 5RL, UK

www.swansignatures.co.uk

978-1-915608-01-7   Paperback
978-1-915608-02-4   Hardback
978-1-915608-03-1   Ebook

Cover design by www.team-design.co.uk

Cataloging-in-publication record for this book is availiable from the
British Library.

Contents

The Gift of Giving

Muzahid Khan

Chapter One: Childhood

The world of my birth

I was born in December 1969, in a village called Singerkach, just thirty kilometres away from Sylhet. Sylhet is one of the major cities in the north-eastern region of Bangladesh and gives its name to the entire division. Situated on the bank of the Surma River, Sylhet can lay claim to being the most important city in the country after Dhaka and Chittagong.

But I was born before Bangladesh – as its own country – even existed. The tensions between the then East Pakistan and West Pakistan, separated by more than 1300 miles, had been brewing for some time and when I was just a one-year-old the Liberation War began. The West Pakistani army invaded East Pakistan and killed people based on either their religion, or opposition to West Pakistan. There were a lot of inhumane actions taking place - murders, rapes and looting. The villagers were terrified. Everyone feared that if the Pakistani army came into the village, they would kill indiscriminately. That fear was enough to drive people out of their homes and keep moving, keep moving, until they felt safe.

Many people went to other towns and cities, but our family remained in villages. That doesn't mean we remained in the same place, we still had to move around different villages. Amazingly, the army never came as far as our village.

Of course, I can remember none of that time, but my Mum told me a story about how they had to carry me as a little baby, fleeing to a neighbouring village to ensure that we were safe from the Pakistani army. They fled across several rivers and fields to get to a neighbouring village and, thankfully, we all arrived safely. It was in this village, Singerkach, about thirty kilometres outside of Sylhet, where I was raised. At that time, I was the only child in our family and in our village. Thankfully, not many people were affected in that village, as they were elsewhere, because of the war.

My mum and grandma would always tell me stories about those harrowing times. How they used to fear for their lives, how there was scarcity of food, and how keeping me alive was their top priority. I thank these women for their resilience and for their love. Because of them, I am here today. Being just a small village on the outskirts of Sylhet, Singerkach had no proper roads. People would travel by boat or use dirt-track roads. There were not many vehicles, so people used to walk for miles and miles regardless of the weather. Whether it was raining, monsoon, or extremely hot weather, people would walk to wherever they needed to get to.

If you can imagine, Sylhet, the only main town or city in the area, was still not properly developed. If people needed to go and visit a medical facility, then Sylhet town would have been the only place with any reasonable facilities. However, during the Liberation War, anybody who had any form of illness or injury would not have been able to access any health facility. Unless there was some natural remedy available to cure whatever was wrong with them, they would often be left to die wherever they were.

Village Life

I don't remember much about the Liberation War, so my earliest recollections of growing up in the village were very happy ones. I lived there with my Mum, Grandmother and my uncles. My Father was in England collecting funds to send back to Bangladesh during the Liberation War. He was very active in Greater Manchester under the leadership of Abdul Motin of Manchester. My father and his peers would spend many nights having meetings, organising and participating in demonstrations in Oldham, Manchester and London. He was a very patriotic person and played his part from the United Kingdom as a Mukti Judda – a freedom fighter. He also provided for us from there, initially working in a cotton mill.

I fondly recall the happy memories of growing up in the village, where I stayed up to the age of seven and a half. I remember running to the paddy fields with tiffins full of food for my uncles who worked there. They would plough the fields with two cows, and once they had finished, they would sit down in the aisles of the paddy fields and eat. I would eat with them instead of coming back home, which was really fun and exciting for me as a small boy. When they had finished, I'd bring the tiffins back home and let them carry on with their work.

Many a time I would want to take part in the muddy fields. It was so much fun getting mud all over you as you walked around the paddy field, shouting at the cows and making a special noise that would help them move along. It was a bit dangerous for a kid, I guess, but I enjoyed standing next to my uncle and walking along as the rake cut into the mud, making the field fertile and ready for planting. Later on, I also joined my uncles to sow the seeds into the field and I would watch the seedlings grow over time. I did this while I was at school, I was probably about six because it was just a couple of years before we came to England.

After a month or so, the rice crop was ready to harvest. We'd do it by hand, of course, with a sickle. We'd cut the rice and then bundle it up, then bring the bundles back to the village farmhouse. One of the most enjoyable times I remember was that at night-time they would use the cows to grind the rice seed from the husk, and during this process the men would sing songs to stay entertained.

We would get all sorts of people from different houses coming and helping out. You'd have the cows treading the harvested rice crop to separate the grain, and people would sing. There'd be food cooked and it was always a nice summer evening. The crops would be separated and put into bags to be used for when winter came. Throughout the year then, you'd have enough rice bags in the house. I enjoyed all of this.

During the monsoon season there would be water everywhere, from what it seemed to me as a kid, anyway. Water would even come up to the veranda of the house, so if we had to go out, we had to get in a little boat. To go to the bazaar, or go to my maternal grandma's house - my Nani's house. The waters would flood the fields and submerge the roads.

My uncles would prepare for fishing because at that time the fresh water was very clean. They would do it at night and they would catch so much fish, it was amazing. All the villagers would do the same, catching fish all-night and bringing in buckets or baskets full to the brim into their houses. As the water subsided, they'd place handmade wooden baskets along the river where the water was going down to catch fish. The water would flow and fish would go with it, getting caught in the basket.

They caught so much fish that it was really fun for a young child. Much of the fish would be cooked and eaten though a certain portion would be dried and salted, to be eaten at any time in the near future as dry fish.

For those few years after the Liberation War, we didn't have radio or TV. If there was a government announcement or news, we'd have a guy who would travel through the villages on a rickshaw, shouting out what it was with a microphone. You see in the movies the Mughals communicated by having messengers go to villages and read out a statement. It was a bit like that. Sometimes you'd get messages pinned on the wall in the bazaars for people to read, and other times you'd get someone on a rickshaw going around telling people if there was bad news or things they needed to be aware of.

When the war ended, life for our village just went back to normal really. I never heard any particular stories of the aftermath other than the fact that there were food shortages, and that people were still afraid because of the stories they had heard from neighbouring villages. It was not fear of people being killed after the war, but just that so many people had lost their lives during the war that the reverberations carried on even after Independence was announced. People were still very anxious and apprehensive - what if they come back? There was no way of knowing, no daily communication. You had to wait for a bit of information to come from somebody who had a radio or some government sent people on rickshaws.

In our village everybody was supporter of Sheikh Mujibur Rahman - affectionately known as 'The Father of the Nation' or most commonly, Bongabondhu (Friend of Bengal). Pretty much everybody was in unison about independence. They were very excited that Bongabondhu had led their revolution to create independence and, quite genuinely, everybody was on the same page. Obviously, as time has progressed, people have given allegiance to different political parties, but at the time everybody in my village - whether they were Hindu or Muslim - were of that opinion. As I was growing up, I never heard any stories of individuals or families that were against independence.

Although village life was fun for a child, it wasn't for the adults. There were many struggles with ensuring that we had enough food. I'm sure there were moments when we were very short on food, the harvests weren't as good, and the money wasn't coming from England fast enough. In those days, it wasn't like you just pressed a button and then receive the money at the other end.

Another struggle was when my grandma, my Dad's mum, died. I think she died from diarrhoea because there was no treatment back then. If we had known then what we know now, she may not have died so soon. Medical treatment was quite primitive or non-existent. When I was a child I got sick one time and I was taken to the doctors in Sylhet, but they couldn't cure it. My mum and dad found an herbalist who used to work in another village from a different district. He used some leaves and other natural ingredients to create a herbal remedy. I was cured after that.

In return for saving my life, my mum gave him her gold necklace. It was a gift, a form of payment, and a thank you. For my mum nothing was more precious than her son, her own flesh and blood. I reflect on the sacrifices she made for me and always feel that I have not managed to repay her, other than give her the love, affection and comfort that she deserves.

School Days

I have fond memories of going to the local primary school of my village. That said, I didn't really enjoy the studying bit at school itself! My father was an educated man, so it was expected of me to study as well. I used go to Singerkach Primary School along with perhaps thirty to forty children from different villages.

I'm pretty sure my school had a tin roof, though I struggle to remember whether it was half brick half tin, or if it was all tin, but today it is all brick.

It was one long room where all children would stay. We'd sit on benches and have slate boards to write on with chalk. At that time, it was a privilege having slate boards at all! We'd do a lot of rote learning, and for whatever we needed to learn, we would practice it on the slate with a piece of chalk. School days weren't very long so as long as you had learned something that day, you knew you were on the right path. Because it was a rural and farm-like area, a lot of the children would run off to the paddy fields after school had ended to see their uncles and fathers working. They would go looking for food and entertainment.

Doing sports activities would also make school life interesting. We would run around, play games, and just be naughty. We had mixed ages classes, meaning that teachers would teach, more or less, the same material regardless of the age. Children would have been around six to ten years old, so the age difference wasn't that vast. Kids who had advanced would move on from class one to class two, then class three, four and so on. Classes were usually small, even when we were all together.

The age of the children didn't matter, they wouldn't move on until they'd learned enough and passed the end of year tests. Some kids would still be in class one if they hadn't learnt the required syllabus properly, like the alphabet and so on, even if they were older than most of the class. I remember quite a few older kids being in my class one, perhaps because their learning ability was not as fast as the others'.

Dangers and superstitions

Sometimes I'd run off to my Nani's house and pretend I went to school instead. If she wasn't happy that I was skipping school, then I would run to the bazaar to hide from family. There, I would just play with other kids.

The bazaar was set up specifically near this big river that surrounded the village so people could come in their boats. The river was known as the makunda nodi. Not only would they come in boats, but there were also steamboats, or 'launches' as they called them. They would go up and down the river, from one part to the other, taking people all the way to Sylhet. We enjoyed running along the edge of the river to watch these steamboats coming in and bringing lots of people, then picking up some others and move onto the next village after folks had done their shopping.
I remember when I was around six years old, I tried to catch a steamboat by running off the riverbank edge. I fell off and went straight into the river. Thankfully, I didn't get caught up in the moving propellers of the steamboat, otherwise I probably wouldn't be here to tell this story now!

However, this wasn't the only time I put myself in danger. At that time, cars were scarce in my village, at its best, we would see one once a month. Because of this, children would get excited at their appearance and go running after them. As they drove through the field, I would run along the older kids, trying to catch them. One day, I actually managed to catch one. I jumped on the back of the truck, and it took me far away.

My family was very worried, everybody was out looking for me, but they couldn't find me. Thankfully, I only went as far as the nearby village, about four or five kilometres away from my village. One of my cousins was a merchant and happened to be in the bazaar of that village. He found me and brought me home. If he hadn't been there, who knows if anyone would have found me, or what would have happened to me. That was a scary moment for my family, but I can only remember bits of it now, like jumping on the back of that vehicle.

The harsh reality of village life is that sometimes such dangerous moments do end in tragedy. I didn't see any myself, but I used to hear regularly of children drowning. With the area being very rural, we also frequently used to hear that the koopibag - which is like a tiger - used to take kids away. It used to roam around and if a child was left unattended away from the uthan, or if there were no adults around, then it would attack and take them away.

I also used to hear that quite a lot that people were bitten by snakes, mostly on roadsides and at night. At that time, the only remedy for snake bites was to bring in healers and have them chant all night around for the patient. These healers would bring their drums and sing all night. I think these healers were called the Ujja. They'd sing for days and nights to try and sing away the poison. When the singing didn't work, then they would use a horn to suck out the poison and paint themselves with it.

I once saw it with my own eyes. Because of my young age, I wasn't normally allowed to witness these kinds of things, but once in a while, my uncle and would take me with him and let me watch it. I must admit, the singing was really nice, though I wasn't sure of its medicinal effectiveness on releasing poison from somebody's leg! The whole process was fun to watch because it was a very theatrical, but of course, it wasn't fun for the one suffering with the snake poison.

It would have been more useful if they'd done the sucking as soon as the person was bitten, rather than after the singing, but there was a lot of superstition. Of course, village life would not be village life without superstition! I remember we would also paint a black dot on the side of the head of new-born babies to ward off evil.

We also had a superstition linked to one of the ponds in our area. It was said that the pond was cursed, and that in fourteen generations, the pond will be released from its spell and a boat full of gold will rise. Well, if that is to come true, we will have to wait another ten generations!

Our family believed the story of the curse because every so often, my grandmother would lose her senses and go running to the pond, trying to jump in it. My uncles and aunties would wrestle with her because they believed that she was possessed by the demon in the pond. They used to say that when they wrestled with her, she had the strength of four men.

Village Life

Sports were important to me very early on in my life, as they usually are for most village boys. I used to play a lot of football and we had to make our own ball out of hay. We would roll the hay until it was the right size and then tie it up with a string. It was all we had and we were happy enough with it.

Then, my father sent me a football from England, and it made me very proud as I was the only child in the village with a football. I only invited my closest friends to our farmhouse to play with the ball. I would carry it under my arm and take it everywhere I went. To my grandma's house, along the road to the bazaar, etc. I used to show it off to people saying things like "I have a football!"

We played with the football a lot, but sadly someone kicked it into a bunch of thorns, and it popped because it wasn't really a leather ball, but a plastic one. This happened within a few months of getting it and that was it really, my proud moment fizzled away by thorns!

Around the ages of five or six, I used to spend a lot of time in my maternal grandma's house. I would go to her place almost every day, because she loved me very dearly and her house wasn't very far from our place. She didn't have any boys in the family, there were only girls, my aunties, so she was really happy to have a grandson. I would visit her every day, and go to the bazaar and to do her shopping for her.

I remember one time she gave me money to buy something, but I didn't bring any change back. I didn't know how much money I had, but I mistook it for something less than what I actually had. I gave it all to a fishmonger, who didn't give me any change back. When I came back, my family were all like, "Okay now where's the money? Where's the change?" I responded, "He didn't give me any change". So, my Nani sent some men to find this fishmonger. They went to the market asked me to point him out, so I did. They had to shake him up a bit to get the change off him!

After shopping in the bazaar, I would return to my maternal grandma's house in the evening and I would gather all the children from neighbouring houses. We'd sit there reciting Islamic surahs or verses as the sun went down. We'd all sit on a bench and chant in our loudest voices. Sometimes we'd sing the Bangla songs, shouting at their loudest and singing as much as possible. That was such fun and so enjoyable.

During the monsoon season, there were a lot of thunderstorms. We'd stay in the house while the storms raged outside. Outside my grandma's house, there used to be a lot of mango trees, so during these storms we would listen to how mangoes would fall on the tin roof, making loud banging noises. We'd wait for the rain to ease off so we could run out to gather them and bring them to eat. I always remember those times with excitement.

When hailstorms came, they would bring huge hailstones, that would sometimes dent or make hole in the tin roof. Water would come pouring in, but as a child, it all seemed exciting fun. However, I'm sure it wasn't fun for the adults.

Back then, the houses in the village were mainly built with mud-thatched walls and sand, cement, and bamboo pillars. If your roof was made out of tin, then you would be alright. The alternative would be straw made out of rice shoots. The straw would be bundled up and used to secure the roof. These strawroofed houses tended to be made by people who had no income source and couldn't afford tin roofs. A lot of people who had family members in Britain were able to afford tin roofs. Some others, who received a little more money, would also have walls made out of tin.

In those days, it was rare to see a house made from bricks and cement. Over time this has changed, of course. It has been mainly through the economic impact of migrants who brought money back into the community, that villages like ours have prospered and developed.

Most of the villages would still have been in a similar position to ours, or one or two maybe better. The rest were still emerging with people who were going to work in England. My father helped many people from our village to get a job in the cotton mills of England. There was a huge need for labour because locals weren't interested in working there.

Originally, our family lived in the traditional set up of houses, with shared uthan and ponds. Eventually, we came to have our own individual farmhouse, it was bought with the earnings of my uncle Abdul Subhan Khan and my father. The land around it included two ponds, and we didn't have to share them, nor the common courtyard, the uthan, with anybody else. Just our family - my grandma, my uncles and a couple of my aunties who weren't married by then. We were essentially one extended family.

However, majority of people in the village would be sharing one courtyard and one pond with four or five different families. Whereas we had two ponds, one at the front, and one at the back. Our space was bigger and private. Now that the village is too congested, people have moved out of the shared spaces to buy land and build their own homes. Everybody has a brick house now, which is a sign of how migration has affected the economics of the area in forty years.

My Parents

My father was educated up to the age of eighteen and reached matriculation level (the equivalent in Bangladesh of the British GCSE system). He used to live in Bishwanath, which is about ten kilometres from us. He studied at the high school there and was really a bright student. His mathematics skills were sometimes more advanced than even the teachers! He was a bit of a maths genius really, I used to hear stories of how he would catch out teachers' mistakes at maths work.

His mum died while he was doing his matriculation exams. He was busy studying, and she didn't want to interrupt his studies to come home, so she didn't let him know she was struggling. It was a very sad moment for him.

Years after he finished Matriculation, he became a teacher in a secondary school in Mirpur, Jagannathpur. Because of his education, he was also able to build a secondary school in the village, being him the main coordinator of the project. He gained support from local people as well as people from abroad who sent money to create and build the school. To this day, he is referred to as the founder of the school, and many students have gone onto brilliant careers because of this opportunity of education. He believed that without education and without the school, the future of the area would have been bleak. After building the school, he came to England to join his brother and cousins who were already in the UK.

On the other hand, my Mum only went to primary school. Shortly after that, she got married to my Dad at an early age, which was common at that time. Before they got married, my Dad came to England. Over the years, he had helped a lot of people fill in their voucher forms to come to England. He was always the one filling these forms but he didn't want to come to Britain himself. It was my grandmother who pushed him and said, "You know you need to go for the sake of the family, to be able to earn more!" So, although he didn't want to, he came. He first came to Northampton, then Halifax, and finally Oldham where he joined his cousins. He actually ran away from Halifax to Oldham hoping to go back to Bangladesh because he didn't like the cold! Such is the irony of all this that, I don't like the cold either, even after all these years.

He stayed in Oldham for a while, working in some mills. He then went back to Bangladesh and married my mum. She was only primary-school educated, and like all girls, she had been brought up from very early on to think and act like a housewife. She was a clever woman who managed to run a good house for many years, raising the children and looking after the family.

She was the backbone of every success that has happened in the family, including with my father's achievements in England and Bangladesh. She was a good partner who my father could rely on to give him the space he needed to support and help people in Bangladesh and Oldham.

After getting married, he came back to England but didn't bring my mum with him. In his mind's eye, he wasn't going to stay in the UK long term. He wanted to go back like most men who went back to Bangladesh after working for a few years in England. That's why he didn't think it was necessary to bring his family with him. It was only after I was born, he went back to Bangladesh. My grandmother pressured him saying, "Take your family! Make a better life for them over there and just send us money to look after us here."

I guess because of that he decided to bring us, my mum, my brother, and me. That was in 1978, and my younger brother, Moshahid Khan, was part of the liberation movement in England during the liberation war. He was gaining support, collecting money, organising meetings, going to demonstrations and things like that.

Last Days in Sylhet

I was almost eight years old when the time to leave for England came. I was quite naughty at that time. I would tell the schoolteachers in my village "You won't be able to shout at me anymore. I am going away!" I also used to go around the bazaar telling people that I was going to London. For us, London was England. London was the brand name and the whole country; nobody knew what England was. If you were going to London, it meant you were privileged and that you were going for a better life. You'd become wealthy in more ways than one. And so, on July the 30th 1978, we boarded an aeroplane at Dhaka and we flew to London.

Chapter Two: UK and the 80s

Leaving Bangladesh

Those last few days were really very exciting for me as a child. Going to London felt like an adventure. We were going to a better life, where everything was going to be rosy and the streets would be paved with gold! You pictured London, imagining all the best things and thought "Wow! What a privilege". "I am going to experience something that no one else in the village has experienced." I was full of adrenaline and energy.

At the same time, my Nani was very upset. She thought, 'I'm going to lose my grandkids to a foreign land. How are they going to survive? Are they going be able to get the right kind of food? And what if they never come back? What will happen to them?' She was very upset and anxious, and even said to my mum, "You know, go for two months and then come back." One side of the family was like 'take your family for a better life', but the other was anxious about us going away to another country where everything would be different.

My Dad didn't come to Bangladesh much, but he came when it was time to take his family to England. That day came was very emotional. Everybody was crying as we said goodbye, there was really proper wailing going on. We got to Dhaka and stayed in a hotel. Going to the city for the first time was all new to me, and everything seemed huge. We were only there for maybe twenty-four hours but I got to picture the city like in the song, 'the city with the red, blue and green lights'. It was full of lights and colour, contrary to the village with no electricity or running water. In the village, we only had kerosene lanterns, so when I saw the city lit up like people would say, I thought, 'wow! This is really, really amazing!'

This was July 1978, only seven years after the war. Back then, Dhaka was still small and recovering from the destruction of the Liberation War. Because we were only there for twenty-four hours, we really didn't get to see much of it. We mostly stayed in the hotel and didn't go outside much. Looking at Dhaka then and looking at Dhaka now, everything is completely different. It's much more developed and much more culturally advanced. There's also a lot more people and congestion than back in 1978.

I went back to Dhaka in 1996 on a tour with British professionals. There was about twenty of us who went over to visit educational institutions, health centres, government departments, and police headquarters in Dhaka. We met lots of ministers and went to various villages, including my own. Our intent was to give the British professionals practical experience and a sense of the Bangladesh diaspora and culture. This would help them organize their services and gain a better understanding of the community they were serving in the UK. We moved freely around the city and were welcomed with open arms everywhere we went, we even joined Dhaka University in their celebration of the victory day. I took some videos of Dhaka back then, and now that I watch them, I can say that Dhaka in 1996 and Dhaka in 2020 are completely different.

Dhaka has mushroomed into such a big metropolis with buildings everywhere and so many people. There is so much hustle and bustle, and economic and cultural activity everywhere. There is no trace from the battered and left ruined place from years ago.

Anyway, once our twenty-four hours were up, we were whisked away in a bus to the airport. I remember walking on the track going to the aeroplane. I'd walked so fast that I'd left my parents behind. I was near the steps and I looked up at all these people, but they weren't my parents. I thought, 'Oh my God I've lost my parents!' I had to go back down the line looking at each family until I found mine. Then, I just pretended that I had always been there, as if I hadn't been missing for a while.

We got on the aeroplane and I had a pocketful of marbles my Nani gave me to play with while I was in England. But then the aeroplane took off at a very steep angle, and all the marbles fell out of my pocket. They rolled all the way down to the bottom of the aeroplane, so I lost them all! It was a long flight, but I was asleep for most of the time. I don't remember much of the journey, other than losing those marbles.

Arriving in England

We arrived at London Heathrow. From the windows of the airport I saw all these black cars lining up outside. I was told they were called 'black cabs'. There were hundreds and hundreds of them outside.

We were picked up by my dad's friend, Mr Shomuz Miah. He was probably one of very few people at the time who had a car. I'm guessing it was a Datsun, a popular model at the time. On our way to Oldham, we stopped at a place which I later got to know as a 'service station'. We were hungry, so we stopped to have some food. This was my first encounter with the well-known British meal - beans on toast! We ordered tea and beans on toast, but I found I didn't like its taste. My mum and I struggled with this food because we had never tasted it before, and we couldn't finish ours. We regularly eat beans on toast now, but at the time, it was foreign and difficult to digest.

Finally, we arrived at Oldham, it was a sunny summer day. As we walked into the house we were going to live in, I saw a bike in the yard. I'd never seen one before, so I took it and tried to ride it without anyone's help. Of course, I fell straight away.

The house we were going to live in was owned by another uncle who was already there with his family. It was a two-bedroom, terraced-brick house. It had a front room, a kitchen, two bedrooms upstairs, a gas fire downstairs, and a toilet outside.

There was my uncle, his wife and two of his boys before we came. Then another uncle came, he was single. You can probably imagine how squeezed we were in that house! When it was time to sleep, my uncle and his family would stay in the big room, and my family in the small room. My other uncle had to turn the front room into a makeshift bedroom at nights, and would probably end up sleeping on the floor. There was only one toilet outside, so obviously we had to queue up for it or time things right so that you could get to the toilet quickly.

We settled in and adjusted to the house and routine, but it was difficult because we were so squashed. You can imagine how it was during meals or when trying to use the bathroom! Luckily it was summer when we moved, so there was no need for heating, but when winter came, we faced some difficulties. There was only one gas fire in the front room, so we had to huddle up together all the time. We only had one black and white TV too. It was before Channel Four even existed, so it only had three channels. I remember watching Coronation Street on my first days. I had never seen a TV before, so I was fascinated by it. I strongly remember wondering 'how is it possible there are people inside a box, moving, walking around, talking? Is that a cat on the yard roof?' It got me thinking about how this technology worked, and I would end up going to look at the back of the telly, really trying to find where the moving people were.

On the other hand, adults had to go to work in the mills. They were working day and night shifts, so they weren't in the house half of the day. On the weekends, the men would go to the farm to do some shopping. They'd bring back live chickens, and we'd prepare them in the yard. I know that's not going to sound too good to vegetarians, but that's how it was done back then.

In my first weekend, my uncle took me to Oldham Town Centre, which wasn't really much of a town centre back then. He took me to a sports shop and bought me a jersey, shorts, socks and trainers for me to play in. He also bought sportswear for my brother, and we were really pleased with these gifts.

Community Spirit in Oldham

In those days, there were many families coming over from Bangladesh with very little English. Women, in particular, would often have no language at all. Coming from rural villages, like my mum, they had little access to education. To help them, there used to a programme to teach English at homes. Women would get together in a house and an English teacher would come to teach them. My mum and my aunties, like many other women, used to go to these sessions to learn English. Some of the women are in their 70's now, and continue to use the language they had learned years ago.

There's a strong and well-established Bangladeshi community in Oldham. It has grown over the decades, but even back then, there were only a few of us, so we tried to stick together.

There was a bit of an enclave where a lot of Bangladeshi families had bought houses close to each other. Mars Street, Osbourne Street, Quebec Street, were a few of them. In the row of houses of our street, out of six or seven houses, only two were owned by white families, and when my father bought our first house, he bought it two doors away from the house we first came to, in that same row of seven houses. I'm not sure how much it cost, but it was probably around £1,400.

Still, we were a very small community. By around 1991 we were around two and a half thousand people, but in the 80s it probably would've been around a thousand or thousand and a half maybe.

Everyone knew everyone, which was amazing. It was pretty much like an extended family. We would welcome newcomers and even do farewell dinners for those who returned to Bangladesh. When somebody new arrived in England, people would invite them to eat in so many different houses and give them gifts. It would be the same thing if you were leaving UK. They'd feed you and you'd go around a lot of different families saying goodbye. It was a nice atmosphere, and the community was so respectful. We truly shared genuine emotional connections.

There was one time when we had an Eid prayer in a hotel ballroom, and everybody who went there already knew each other, which was nice. On Eid days, boys would go to the park wearing their nice clothes and have fun.

One of the other memorable experiences in the 80s was watching Indian movies. You'd hire out a video player and get six Indian films, which was the usual package. You'd get the video player and six movies, but you only had 24 hours to watch them, and each one was three hours long! 18 hours total. My father didn't allow us to watch Indian movies or get a video player in the house, so I used to go to some other friend's house and watch movies with their families on their days off. They'd watch the six movies back-to-back with maybe a couple of hours sleeping in between. I used to go and watch at least one or two with them. I'd sit on the floor of the front room and watch these movies with them.

My generation, particularly in Oldham, grew up on a staple diet of Indian movies. We watched their films and listened to their music, so we became fluent in the language. We'd look at Indian movie stars and many of us saw them as aspirational figures and role models.

My children's generation absolutely don't go anywhere near Indian movies. I think their generation are more into modern western stuff. Kids are culturally diverse now, following American or Islamic culture. There has been definitely a shift, for quite a number of kids, their influences would vary from Islam, or Bangladeshi culture, but the vast majority would probably be influenced by American and social media culture.

The Bangladeshi community wasn't the only community in Oldham, of course. There were small groups of Indian communities, and the Pakistani community was even larger than the Bangladeshi. Where I lived, there were only one or two Pakistani families, they lived in different areas, which to this day, has prevailed its geographical demarcations. Even now, the Pakistani community is slightly larger in this town.

While tensions still rose sometimes in Bangladesh over the Liberation War and Pakistan's role, it was a little different in the UK. To be honest, it was like a two-sided coin. Everything on the surface was civil, people were getting on and had their own issues to tackle. Labour, protests against racism, the economy, and just adapting to life here kept them busy. The agenda was slightly different here, you had very little time to think about 'do I like this person or not '. But it was a two-sided coin because both communities, especially the Bangladeshis, couldn't forget what Pakistan, their leader and their army had done. People still had political views in the UK, but the inner feelings of both sides were kept silent for a long time. If people wanted to talk about their views, they had to do it in their own groups.

Bongabondhu was assassinated in 1975. I was six years old, so I don't remember any of what happened at the time. Zia was elected in 1977. My father came to Bangladesh that year, just before Zia was elected, and took us to England in 1978. I don't remember when Zia was assassinated in Chittagong either. It was May 1981, so I was in the UK by then. There must have been ripples of shock in the communities considering how important and influential these two leaders were, but I don't remember any of that. In those days, news broadcasting wasn't that clever. If my father had heard about it through a phone, it wasn't really a conversation that I would have been part of.

School Days

I went to St. Hilda's primary school, which was about half a mile away from my house, so I always used to walk there. Unfortunately, the area we lived in was rather derelict and dilapidated back then, with lots of empty, falling-apart properties. As children we used to go and play inside them. Looking back at it now, it was very risky because if you fell through one of the boards, or got hit by something, you could have easily been knocked out or gotten injured.

When we'd walk to school, there were times we'd be chased by white boys. It was fun for them to pick on brown boys and girls, so we always went in a cluster to make sure we'd be safe. Even though it was half a mile or so, there were still people out there who wanted to chase you and give you a good hiding. They were difficult times.

I remember when I took part in the primary school nativity play; I was one of the kings. The nativity plays were at night and in winter, and I had to go to school on my own, so it was quite scary. I would run as I fast I could from my house to the school so that nobody could see me or catch me. After the play I'd also run straight back home in the dark, fearing that I was going to be caught by some of the other older lads who wanted to beat up a brown kid. I didn't look left or right, I just made one big dash, a half a mile run, probably my fastest runs ever.

However, I must admit that most white kids were very friendly with me at school. I played with them after school as we were part of the football team. That's where I got to make friends with quite a number of white kids.

We also used to go swimming and go cross-country running. I was one of the two Asian kids in the cross-country team, and we used to go cross-country running with the school in the evenings. Again, it was really scary catching the bus back because you didn't know when you were going to get beaten up. This worry was always, always in the back of my mind, 'When am I gonna get beat up?'

We didn't have enough money, so I remember going to school with a hole in my shoe. When it rained, the water would seep into the hole and my sock would get really wet. I used to cut a piece of cardboard and put it into the sole to cover the hole. These are the kind of memories that help you stay grounded, shape your development and make you appreciate your improvement in life. It's great to tell these stories to your children, they're never going to believe you because everything is so different now.

School was difficult because I didn't understand English, so I was buddied up with the other Bangladeshi kids. There were only five or six children of Bangladeshi origin and one of them was tasked to show me around and make feel at ease. His name was Mashukul Hoque, and to this day he remains one of my closest friends.

I remember my first reading in front of the teacher. I didn't understand most of the words in the text, but there were two particular words I really didn't get. The first one was 'greenhouse', I thought it was a house painted green! The other one was 'sandwiches', which I thought were witches made out of sand.

You can imagine a kid coming into a new environment with a new language and culture... Clearly it was going to take a long time before I could fully grasp these new societal norms. There was definitely a clash in my head, a cultural clash between my own culture and what I had grown up with at home, and the new culture I was beginning to embrace. You may say it was an identity crisis of sorts.

Racism

When we lived on Mars Street we used to get our windows broken every other night. There used to be a group of young, thuggish kind of characters that wandered around the neighbourhood chucking bricks or stones at windows. We always feared that this would escalate to a much more dangerous situation. This continued for years, even after we moved to our house, four doors away in the same street. At nights, dogs would be barking outside, and men would have to keep an eye out, watching the streets. Police would also be frequenting the area.

Even in Ramadan you couldn't eat and break the fast in peace, because the lads would want to cause a nuisance and throw a brick at your window. We had to live through all that. I remember my mum used to keep a suitcase packed because we thought that one day we might get bombed or attacked in such a way that we'd have to flee. I don't know where we would have gone, maybe somewhere else in England, or maybe we would have left for good, back to Bangladesh. We always used to live with that fear, and I guess it caused a bit of trauma for us, because even years later wherever we went, we were still cautious that we might get picked on, whether by racist remarks or physical attacks, which were really bad when they did happen.

One time my younger brother actually got hit in the face on the doorstep got picked on in the streets a couple of times, but, you know, because I used to run quite a bit, I managed to stay away from them. We also had to be cautious whenever we went into town. We used to fear going into some areas, even if they were only half a mile down the road. We knew there were certain areas which were no-go for us, it was all quite traumatic.

In the 80s there were a lot of National Front marches in Oldham, and I remember that my dad and other men would organize counter-marches. They would go into town and we would hear stories about how they were preparing themselves. I remember hearing that one of the men in our house was carrying chilli powder in little sacks, so if they got attacked, he would throw chilli powder at the faces of the racists. These men were all very well supported by the community, and they remained active for a number of years.

It was the late 70s or early 80s, and I remember being interviewed with my father on one of the northern TV channels. The reporters wanted to know about the everyday racism. I was about 10 or 11 at the time; it was really frightening.

Getting used to English Life

We struggled during winter, and in the 1980s, the UK had some terrible winters. It was really bad, to the point where we couldn't go outside be-cause it was severely cold. I had never experienced that kind of winter in Bangladesh, the kind of winter where it snows for weeks on end. As you can imagine ,the worst part of all was going to the outdoor toilet. You had to fight your way through piles of snow and then when you got to the toilet it was absolutely freezing to sit on it. It was quite a struggle in those days, and compared to it what we have now is an absolute privilege.

We used to have a bath once a week. There is a place called The Robin Hill and my father would take us there with the boys to the public baths. We'd get a room with a bath and had an hour to clean ourselves and get out. But because we were all individually placed, I was so scared my Dad was going to leave us all or I that wouldn't be able to find him, that I used to come out after just ten or fifteen minutes of using the bath. However, I soon realised that I shouldn't do that because we paid for an hour, so we should stay in there for as much of it as possible.

I also used to accompany my father on Saturdays to the public launder-ette for all the washing. We put the coins into the machine, made sure that our clothes were properly washed, then put them in a dryer before putting them back in the carrier bags and bring them home.

The area where we were living while I was growing up had quite a few farms. The farms would have these apple trees, but obviously we weren't allowed to take any apples from the trees. I had a group of friends, some younger, some older and some with similar age, and we'd go for a walk around the farms, looking at the cows and horses and when nobody was looking, we'd take some apples from the trees. We used to sit on the fields and have some of those nice apples. It was definitely fun!

There was a little park near our house which we used to frequent, it was called Berries Field. Most evenings the Bangladeshi boys would gather here because there was nowhere else to go. They'd play football, cards, run around or just like wrestle each other. It was a good social activity for the young boys to pass the time.

They also had a football team called 'Azad FC', and it was named after a young guy called Azad who was murdered. They used to play either in the Saturday League or the Sunday League, I'm not sure but I used to go watch them and play with the younger ones in the field.

Years before we bought our own house, we lived in a two-bedroom house that again, would be shared with another family. We rented a room in another family's house and it was a similar situation from when we lived with my uncle's family and my other single uncle. By that time I would have been 11-13 years old, and I had to sleep on the sofa downstairs because there was no room or bed for me to sleep in.

At that time my father was the President of the Oldham Bangladesh Association. He was elected in 1978, and that meant frequent meetings in the front room of the house. He also used to fill in people's forms because he worked for manpower services, as opposed to everyone else working in the mills. He would interpret and fill any forms they required, from national insurance forms and benefit forms to housing forms. Basically, he was the man who would help anyone with any need because he was an adviser, and an information worker. Our house then would be an office outside office hours. I would not be able to sleep until late, and then I'd wake up without much sleep, go to school, come back... That went on for years, until I was around sixteen in 1986.

Changing Schools and Further Education

I left St. Hilda's Primary School in 1981 and went to Grange Comprehensive, which was a bigger school. Once again, I didn't face much racism in school because I made friends with most of the key people. One of them was a Bangladeshi boy called Samsul Alam who came into my class six months in. He came from Haslingdon, and he was a big lad. My job was to interpret for him and take him around the school. He was very good at football, so he quickly got into the secondary school football team. As a result, I got to make friends with most of the kids and went through school without any significant difficulty and very little racism, if there was any at all.

He also used to practice karate, so people were very careful not to cause us any trouble or even hint having a prejudice against us. In school there was talk about the possibility of him being part of the 'Cock of the Year' group. In those days, if the word around was that you were the best fighter or the toughest guy in the school, they would call you the 'Cock of the Year' and 'Cock of the School'. However, you had to have a fight with the guy who was the current 'Cock of the Year' to receive this title.

The word got around the school that this Bangladeshi boy was going to fight the Cock after school and see who was the toughest of the two. They had this fight after school, and with Samsul's experience in karate, he kicked the other guy, making him fall and hurt his back. From that day onwards Samsul got maximum respect, and he even became best friends with the previous Cock! Because the two toughest boys became best friends, everything went well and witout any issues for the remaining five years of secondary school.

In one of my classrooms there was a young women who couldn't pronounce my name, so she used to call me Arthur. I was like, 'okay I'll take it if it helps you to get to know me and call me without getting my name wrong. I'll take it'. I bumped into her after almost thirty odd years. It was bizarre to see her after all this time. It remeinded me of the people I used to be friends with. I guess I still see some of them here and there, but there is one particular friend who gives me grief. I heard a few years ago that one of my school friends had died after falling off a balcony in Brazil. This was about ten, fifteen years ago. It was quite sad, and my only memory of him is how he used to call me 'Smelly' in school. When I received this news, either by Facebook or some message, I was quite shaken up and taken aback.

Looking back at those five years of schooling, I realise they were really good. I made lot of friends and was really trying my best to do academically well. Then again, I think I might have been a slow learner at school because it wasn't until I went to Oldham college for the first year of a BTech diploma in business studies that things really started to come together for me. Then, for some reason, I went back and did four GCSEs and the national diploma, but then I thought to myself, 'when am I going to go to University? How will I get there if I keep carrying on being at college?'

I realised that if I didn't get on with it, my brother, who is four years younger than me, would soon be doing his A levels and coming to college himself, and that he'd be ahead of me. So, one summer I decided that in order to get a head start with my academic studies, I needed to read in advance the books that I would be studying the following September. I started studying the books that the teachers were potentially going to use for the subjects in the national diploma, and when I went in September, I fully understood every theory and subject discussed. Everything that was being taught I'd already read about, so I was instantly grasping what the teacher was mentioning. I could visualize it, and it made it so much easier for me to learn. I then went to the University of Salford. That was in the 90s, 1990 I think.

I spent four years at college when I should have only spent two. It was probably because I was still not fully fluent in the language or fully clear on other numerous things of my degree. I realised the only way I was going to succeed was by reading to staying ahead of what the teachers were going to teach and to make sure I understood the language. I was only going to learn the theory if I read extensively, which is what I did. To this day, I still try to read a lot so that I am constantly improving my knowledge.

Chapter Three: 90s

First Employment

After I finished at Oldham college, I went to Salford University, but I left halfway through the first year because my father was ill, which meant I had to get a job. I left the university in 1991 and got a job at the Oldham council as a clerical officer in the treasury department dealing with the poll tax queries among other things.

I worked there for about seven or eight months before I had to take my mum to Bangladesh because my Nani was very ill. I decided to go with my mum because I wasn't sure how long my Nani would be ill and how long we would be required to stay there. My dad couldn't come with us because he was working so he stayed behind and looked after my other siblings. My Nani was very important to me and as the oldest child I took her in and made that sacrifice of leaving my job behind.

Getting to Bangladesh can be expensive and it often makes people wonder how Bangladeshis do this, drop everything to go and look after a sick relative. Sometimes, it is a case of putting something aside for a rainy day. You don't know what that rainy day is going to look like, but you can be prepared for it. Other times, if an emergency does occur and you are not prepared for it, then the rest of the family chip in so you're not as financially burdened as you would be if you had to do it alone. For some, that might be a kind of loan within the family, but with my family most of it is gifting; the gift of giving. Sometimes it can be a loan, when everybody is doing alright you shouldn't be taking gifts, you should give it back. Either way is fine, but most of the time it is gifting.

Handing my notice was a bigger difficulty when going back to Bangladesh. Ceasing working at short notice is something that is almost taken for granted in Bangladesh but really isn't really part of the British culture. In those days. much of the council in Oldham were probably White British people and it may well have seemed strange to them when I said I had to leave for Bangladesh so abruptly. I don't know if it was okay or not but I just went in and said, "I'm handing my notice because I'm going to Bangladesh. I don't know when I'll be back."

They wanted to talk about it, but I'd had enough of working there, so I just wanted to get out. If it had been a job that I thoroughly enjoyed, then it would have been difficult for me to leave and I would have put more effort on leaving them with a positive impression of myself. Luckily, I walked into a job when I got back from Bangladesh.

We stayed in Bangladesh for several weeks, but before going I had had a job interview with the Oldham Muslim Housing Association for a research and development officer role. It wasn't until I was in Bangladesh that I found out through a phone call from my father that I was being offered the job.

Sadly, my Nani passed away. We buried her and at the appropriate time, we came back to the UK. Thankfully, when I got back I was able to take up the job in the Oldham Muslim Housing Association, which was a new organisation back then. I would be one of two employees with the opportunity to develop the organisation, build homes and then rent them out to people from Muslim origins who were living in overcrowded conditions with their large families. I did that for about eighteen months before moving on to work for the Tameside Council in the education department. I worked as a community development worker in the youth and community section working in a predominantly Bangladeshi area of Hyde. The project was called 'Shapla', and my job entailed working with the youth, the elderly and women, to create opportunities and empowerment programs to give them a chance to develop as individuals and within communities.

I was there for a number of years and had the great opportunity to create some very interesting projects with young people, getting them involved in voluntary work, sports, and even employment. I did another eighteen months or so there and then left Tameside in December 1994. At that time my contract had ended and I was about to get married after a lot of planning and organising.

The OBYA

In 1991, a group of young people and I created the Oldham Bangladeshi Youth Association. The organisation was established because there was really nothing for us to do in the area. We thought we, a group of youngsters, could get together and maybe do some activities that would benefit us and the community. We started doing things around the Bangladeshi culture, as this was our strength and identity. We celebrated Independence Day, Bijoy Dibosh, International Language Day and so on. We started with what we knew and what brought people together. We got young children and youngsters to recite poems and perform drama. We designed the stage, spending all night up, building and setting it out. We also organised the kids to practice their performances. It was similar for the adult dramas too, and I even took part in some of them. It was quite a movement because there had been nothing like this here before. Perhaps there was something like this elsewhere in the country, but certainly not in Oldham. It captured the imagination of the entire Bangladeshi community, not only the one in Oldham, but of the Bangla people everywhere. As a result, we ended up doing a lot of cultural projects.

One particularly special project took place in 1992. We created an indoors Shahid Minar, a Bangladeshi monument to the Martyrs. It was made out of wood and it was part of the Bangladeshi Language Day celebrations, also worldwide known as the International Mother Tongue Day thanks to the language martyrs. A lot of people came, so the project was very exciting.

Then the idea progressed to build an outdoor Shahid Minar. This idea was initiated by the Oldham Bangladeshi Youth Association and it was supported and encouraged by many other groups in the community. Eventually, we were able to raise some money and provide resources to build the first ever Shahid Minar outside of Bangladesh, rigth here in Oldham. It is a wonderful thought that we were the initiators of this achievement. I should add that many of the cultural programmes were conceived by Abdu Malik, also known as Master Malik. He was very knowledgeable at matters of Bangla culture, and I am grateful for his involvement.

After that we had the Shahid Minar or the language celebrations outdoors. It would take place on the 21st of February, which meant it was cold and raining sometimes. Nevertheless, it would bring so many people from all around the North West, and even one or two guests from outside the Bangladeshi community because it was seen as the first of its kind. There was an emotional attachment for Bangladeshis here, so when it was launched, it was done with great fanfare. There were hundreds of people that came to the opening, with lot of guests coming from all over the country.

The Shahid Minar was followed by the Shapla project, named after the Shapla roundabout in Dhaka. The public works at the time presented us with a unique, mini, and new roundabout in the area. It was a great opportunity to put a piece of art there and, because it was an area predominantly inhabited by British Bangladeshis, we were able to facilitate the conversation between various groups and authorities to create this Shapla flower on the roundabout. This was another nice little initiative that came out of all the community development activity that went on. This sort of cultural influence enhances the status of an area, and I am proud that I was part of the team that made it happen.

While I was involved in the Oldham Bangladeshi Youth Association, we created a Bangla Summer Mela. These things went on for days with music, art and sports. There were many things engaging young people and families to participate in activities that would be empowering and benefital to them. There was so much fun and laughter, and so many people involved. It was a community festival of culture, and it showed the true essence of community spirit.

Marriage, Children and Promotion!

I got married on Boxing Day December 1994. I would have been around 25 at the time. There is a photo of me with two other young men at that time, we were wearing nice white suits. I think we must have been at a wedding somewhere. In those days, we used to watch a lot of Indian movies, and because of that we would wear a lot of light colour attire. People definitely followed the fashion and music trends of Bollywood, and I have no shame in saying that. Nowadays, a lot of the guys would deny ever watching or having any knowledge of watching Indian movies. But, as much as anyone might deny it, the truth for a lot of people was that their only way of socializing was watching those movies together with someone, getting lost in them.

It was the time in my life where I was transitioning from being free and single, to being married and responsible. All my friends of the same age were married and some were getting married at an even earlier age. I was thinking, 'I'm 24 now. That's about the right time to get married'. I was mentally ready to settle down and take on responsibility. Clearly, I missed the timing because maybe I could have done with a few more years of single life.

The 90s was just a boom decade for me. Not only did I get married and have kids, but I was also having all these different jobs, and getting heavily involved in voluntary and charity work. Day and night, I was always involved in something, which meant I was not a responsible married man as much as I should have been. I tried to balance everything, be active in work, on the voluntary sector, on charity. I think that's what took me away from being more of a family man and spending more time with my family. In the end, we'll see what happens, whether my contributions have made any difference to the lives of people or not, and my family, hopefully, will appreciate that somewhere along the way.

Anyway, I got married in 1994, in Liverpool. I am Sylheti, of course, but my wife is non-Sylheti, which was quite a novelty at the time. We married in Liverpool because that's where she was from, although she actually was born in St Helens. One of several things I liked about her when I first spoke to her was her accent. I was like, 'wow, how different! A Bangladeshi that speaks differently and in a scouse accent!' You can't get a better combination unless you get a Geordie, Or a Glaswegian. She lost that scouse accent in the end!

But there were many things I liked about her. Although she was from liberal family and background, she used to pray a lot. She was very broad-minded, but the one thing that was underpinning all of that, was the fact that religion was at the centre of her life. I thought, 'oh yeah, you know, she's somebody who seems to be all-rounded with good family, good education (she had graduated from her degree), good character and she's got faith as well'. One of the things that my father always used to say was that he didn't mind my wife not being a housewife and working instead. It didn't matter to thim that my wife could be different because the only thing that mattered to him other than the fact that she had strong faith and that she prayed. That was quite cool and quite deep of him as well.

Many of the older people didn't give my marriage a chance, they used to whisper, "he is Sylheti, she is non-Sylheti. He is from the village, she is not." They said that our differences were too big for this marriage to work, and that we would be divorced within six months. They were very testing times, but we had faith and, in the end, you don't get married with the intention to get divorced. If we had relied on culture too much, we would probably have gotten divorced, but instead, we built our marriage on the rules provided by faith. The clear guidance for men and women made us stronger in our marriage.

My marriage was arranged, but I'd met my wife at a dinner where I was selling cookery books for a women's catering collective in Tameside, it was a Bangladeshi collective. I was selling these books for a pound, and by the end of the night, we'd manage to collect a tin full of money. This would enable them take to take driving lessons or something similar. It aimed to be a self-sustaining kind of initiative by these women.

I met my wife at this dinner which was intended for Islamic Studies students at my university, Manchester Metropolitan University. Two of my friends, Phil Buckley and Jon Stonehouse, were on that course. They actually said, "come along, you will get to meet this Bangladeshi lady, and you can even sell your books there."

I went along with my best friend, Kashif Ashraf, and obviously he end-ed up seeing the woman who would be my future wife. When I first saw her I was like 'she doesn't look Bangladeshi!' But then I had a few words with her and realised that she really was from Bangladesh, and that was it really. I didn't see her after that until she came to see a drama I was in. I had given out leaflets for this drama during one of our independence events, 1993 I think. She came with her whole family to watch this drama, and this was the second time I saw her.

Usually when marriages are being arranged and discussed, you need people in the middle of both sides. They would be able to facilitate the conversation, and help reach arrangements that would be appropriate for both sides. However, we didn't have such person at first. I later found a woman named Bella Hoque from Manchester. She was a non-Sylheti woman working in Oldham who could create the connection between the two families, and that's exactly what she did.

Later on, we found out that one of the uncles on her meternal side had been one of my Dad's classmates in Bishwanath. They hadn't seen each other in 30 years, but he was really quite helpful. The chap respected my father and therefore, he was able to facilitate the conversation and make the marriage happen.

Further work opportunities

After marrying, I got another job in Bradford working for the education department in Bradford Council. Again, it was a predominantly Bangladeshi area, and we worked in a project called the Bangladesh Parishad. It was a dynamic initiative with lots of employees looking at a range of different kinds of work that needed to be delivered for that deprived community. The funny thing with was that, initially, I actually didn't want the job. As I was driving to the interview I was thinking, "I don't want this job. What am I doing?' At the interview, I was answered the questions in a very… How can I put it? In a very 'disinterested' way. I didn't care, I didn't want the job!

As it turns out, I had answered the questions in a way that gave them the impression that I was well-organised. They wanted someone strong-minded, and it seemed like I was the right person, so I got the job. During that period, around eighteen months or so, I was moving around a few jobs, and I did this particular job for about six months. I knew I didn't want to stay there anymore because I was facing some difficulties as a manager, so I wasn't really keen to stay there.

I remember one night in 1995, it was snowing and there was a terrible gridlock in Yorkshire, all the way from Leeds to Oldham. I had left the office at five in the evening, but I didn't get home until four in the morning. It took me eleven hours to get back home. Everything was completely jammed because of the snow, it was quite a scary moment really. Fortuately one of those strange moments in life occurred then. In all my life, I had never put a full tank of fuel in the car, but for some completely unknown reason, I had filled the tank full of fuel that morning. This is what helped me to get home safely and without running out of fuel that day.

Soon after, I had to have a hernia operation, so putting these two things together, I just decided I wasn't going back to the job. I returned to Bradford for a few more weeks, or even a month, but after that I left and got a new job in Oldham. I worked as a community safety officer within the new regeneration unit, which had received funding of around £11 million from a single regeneration budget programme. I was blessed with this job and was able to implement a lot of community safety programmes, and a pilot programme before the full community safety unit was set up.

Then, I was promoted! I was put into the main team of regeneration implementation as project officer. I was one of two project officers and worked under the manager. Our job was to manage the programme and do quite a lot of administrative type things. We made sure the area was regenerated, and created a lot of exciting opportunities for the area. It was a very successful programme, it even won a national award called the 'British Urban Regeneration Award in Europe.' That enabled me to move on to another regeneration program called SRB3, Single Regeneration Budget. This project would be in another area, and that area was where the 2001 riots would take place.

The 2001 riots were classed as race riots. The far right, or the National Front, was coming to the town to stir up hate fever. After weeks and weeks of them coming and stirring up hatred, young Asian people decided to retaliate. There was a particular riot that took place over two nights in two different areas of Oldham. The first night was in Glodwick and the second one was in Westwood. All this was televised and beamed across the country and the world. It seemed like the town was burning. Although it took part in a relatively contained space, the street battle was going on for several hours. All of this happened because the National Front was stoking up hate fever. Young Asians, boys especially, refused to take it and sit down peacefully. The whole thing spilt over after many weeks of provocation. People couldn't handle it anymore, and the anger was taken out on the police.

Rich Blessings

My daughter was born in 1997 and my son in 2000. When my daughter was born, she became my lucky blessing, or charm as they say. She brought me good luck, as I was blessed with a promotion in my employment. I also started getting recognition from the Queen and bought our house; it seemed everything was going right for me.

I was also studying part-time for a higher national diploma in Housing at Salford University. I completed that and started studying for a BA

Honours at Manchester Metropolitan University in Business Studies. I had married, I was studying, working, had two children, and was actively volunteering with OBYA. I finally finished my studies in 2020 and got my degree despite all the other things coming into my life, and having these other priorities taking over.

I think it was quite a lucky moment for me because my daughter had been born, my first child. All the family was really happy, and because I had been promoted to the project officer job, we were able to buy a house next door to my parents. We moved into our own little two-up two-down. It was really nice to have a space for my wife, my daughter and myself, and still be next to my parents, because they were very important to me. That luck went on for a good few years.

I received recognition from Her Majesty, The Queen, for being a young achiever. It had to do with the fact that I was working with diverse communities around the North West of England, as well as working with and developing an organisation to bring such diverse communities together. I was among the six hundred young achievers invited to the Buckingham Palace, which was quite a privilege. There, I got to meet some of the famous young names of the time and people that are famous names now.

Then in 2000, I got another invitation to visit former Prime Mininster Tony Blair and his people for doing outstanding work in the community. Nine achievers from each region were invited to attend this ceremony to recognize people who were doing outstanding work or contributions to their community. It was a good opportunity to meet Sir Cliff Richard and other very high-profile people and celebrities. They were a good few days, spending time with the Prime Minister's office and ending with a big event at the Millennium Dome.

The Trips

During the 90s, I started organising trips to Bangladesh, taking British professionals on educational visits. The first one was organised in 1996. I decided I wanted to visit Bangladesh, and I thought what better way to do it than organising an educational tour through the youth organisation. I coordinated and led this trip to Bangladesh for twenty-plus British professionals and young British Bangladeshi people from within our organisations. We went and visited various things that we would normally only have seen on calendars or would have only heard about, like the Bangladesh Parliament, or the actual Shahid Minar. We met ministers and visited government departments, villages, schools, and colleges, all with names that we had only heard as we were growing up. It was really an enjoyable and fruitful trip.

A lot of people who went with me the first time, went again and again, each time with different groups of people. The more of these trips I led, the more skilled I became at organising and managing them, and the more acquainted I got with the key people in Bangladesh. Throughout these experiences, I built relationships with officials from both Bangladesh and British Institutions, making longlasting friendships along the way.

The whole initiative of the travelling continued with various new people joining in each opportunity. We also had people that had gone once or twice before, such as my good friend, Phil Buckley, who went a staggering nine times with me. He didn't miss any of those trips.

I was also part of the Oldham Athletic Football Club, which was the first British Football league club to play friendlies in Bangladesh. Again, whilst I was doing all these trips, I started to connect with the right people in the right places. I also started to better understand the needs of underprivileged people because I was seeing them through the eyes of the visitors. Coming from England, they would see things differently. We had BBC Radio Four come with us and record two documentaries: "Ties that Bind" and "Cementing the Ties". They were looking at the ties that were binding people here in Oldham and back in Sylhet.

Over the years there were many people who came; professional people from schools, colleges, the police force, home office, various politicians, senior officers, and even Radio Four on two occasions. Some of them, specially some of the headteachers, experienced what being looked at meant, being in a goldfish bowl. Whenever these teachers went out with me to visit schools, hospitals, offices, villages, markets, restaurants, or even having a ride on a boat, then, there would be hordes of people looking at them everywhere they went. At moments like these, they would realise what it feels like to be looked at in curiosity by the majority, like how Asian children at their schools would be looked at by white parents, treating them as unusual brown kids. It's almost like being in a zoo.

When I took them to my village, around 500-600 people, if not more, turned up to see these white people with short blonde hair. They were very curious. "Are they really people? Their hair is blonde and their skin white!" People wanted to touch their white skin, but I was very protective of the guests, trying to keep everybody at bay. They finally understood what it meant to be a brown-skinned child of an Asian family coming to their schools. Because of this, they were able to create initiatives and educational processes that enabled a better interaction between the kids and the teachers, as well as getting the families more involved with the school, giving them a space where they would be hopefully understood.

Having visited Sylhet, they understood where their Bangladeshi students were coming from, and they were able to better empathise and talk about things that they had witnessed and seen.

One of the things I particularly remember, is what one of the head-teachers told me when she saw children herding some cows or sheep. I don't know whether they were taking them to the market, or just going home after farming, but the teacher said it reminded her of the story of Jack and the Beanstalk back in England. When Bangladeshi children read the story of Jack and the Beanstalk, they are not that impressed because they've seen children walking cows with their own eyes, so it's no big deal. On the other hand, this image was something new to the teacher.

Initially, the trips were about two weeks long, but then I shrunk them down to ten days as I got better at running them. We spent most of the time in Sylhet, with a day or two in Dhaka, one day on the way in, and a day on the way out. In Sylhet we visited the tea gardens, villages, Jaflong (a famous hill station), schools, colleges, universities, and any other places would be beneficial to my visitors. For this, I would put an itinerary together to keep the travel structured. On the other hand, when we did the cycling tour it was more about seeing some other parts of the country, cycling through various districts, divisions, towns, cities and villages. That tour could be quite a book in itself! However, I shall reduce it to a sole chapter you can read later.

Many interesting things came out of those trips, and at some point we realised that there were divided communities in Oldham, which is something that the 2001 race riots highlighted. There needed to be more integration, so, we created a school-linking project with schools in Oldham and Sylhet. Every year there would be an exchange organized by the council's education department. They would create this exchange programme to bring teachers from Bangladesh for two weeks, give them teacher training, and then they would go back. Teachers from Oldham would also go to Banglaesh and train at the schools there.Similarly, we wanted to create relationships between the schools´ borough so that there would be some form of knowledge sharing and integration going on. Then we wanted the voluntary sector to do that as well, but I guess the riots took over, still, they tried to do it after that.

Sports

In 1999, we went to watch Bangladesh play cricket in their first ever World Cup in Scotland. We were a group of seventy people dressed up in flag drapes covering our bodies, and we spent the first fifteen minutes dancing around outside the stadium. As soon as we got in, we realised Bangladesh was three wickets down, "oh my god, if they are three wickets down in fifteen minutes they could be all out in a couple of hours!" We were quite fortunate that Bangladesh won their first ever World Cup match and that we were there to witness it with our Bangladesh flag and regalia. It was quite an exciting time. We spent hours prancing around in Edinburgh, and when we came back to Oldham, the excitement continued. The OBYA did a lot of football tournaments which brought our communities together. Bangladesh youngsters came from all over the country to Oldham every year to participate. We used to do a national football tournament and it was an opportunity for us to meet people from a similar age group from around the country and see what they were up to, and have a football competition. Football was a great way of uniting people, and a great way of learning new skills, not only on the pitch but when organising and managing people and money. Along with some friends, I organised the first ever six-a-side charity football tournament in 1991 to raise money for the Bangladesh cyclone appeal. This became the annual national seven-a-side football tournament

Similar to the trips, I learnt a lot about leadership, delegation, managing finances, working timetables, and building relationships. For me I think all these experiences have given me what I have today. Organising lots of programmes, events, and trips abroad had the greatest impact in my life. When I first started with the trips, I didn't know anything about Bangladesh. I just took a group of people and they followed me blindly and, thankfully, each trip was successful. There was never a shortage of people that wanted to go with me, and because everybody was paying for themselves, it was just a self-funded trip. I found a lot of satisfaction in knowing that people paid their way out of interest and that it was helpful for them, both individually as people, and in their professions.

I think it was 1996 when we visited the BRACs model village in Narsingdi, Bangladesh, which was visited by the Clintons earlier in the year. We watched how BRAC served the villages with information, helped with education and with microfinance. There would be these champions that would sit on these red motorbikes and act as health or education champions. They'd visit these villages and sit with the families to give them various information. When we got back, the UK Government decided to create a project based on something like that, on community champions. It was a 3-year programme and we could appoint volunteers who would go with a clipboard in hand visiting a block of houses =once a week to give them health, employment or any information they needed. It was a way of engaging better with the community, of empowering them and them into society. They would receive better services by having these volunteers around.

Chapter Four: Giving

The Influence of My Father

While it is very nice to be able to talk about my own life story, really the reason for doing so is to help you, the reader, to understand some of the reasons why I think the way I do. It is these ways of thinking that I truly want to share, believing that they are important ideas which can help anyone who wishes to embrace them. One of the most important ideas I want to share is in the gift of giving.

From an early age I learnt the notion of helping others who are less fortunate and helping people who, with a little bit of support, can improve their lives. When I learnt that notion, it gave me a lot of satisfaction knowing whatever gift I have, I can share some of it, and in that way I can contribute to improving people's lives.

I think the first time I came across the whole notion of giving was from my late father. He dedicated his entire life to improving people's lives - from when he was in Bangladesh to when he came to England. His entire life was devoted to making sure that people were supported in whatever way they needed to be supported. Hence why he moved on from being a mill worker to being an advice centre manager, an advice and information worker, helping people filling in forms and interpreting for them. These were early days in the 70s and 80s for our community, and he was really integral to everything that went on in the community - helping, supporting, giving. He gave a lot to charity himself and, towards the latter stages of his life, he gave from his pension money to support people who were poor.

So, I grew up around this idea of giving: giving of your time, giving of your skill, giving of your money and facilitating others to do the same. Then, of course, the first time I came across quite a big initiative, a fundraising initiative, my father was very involved, along with his friends and colleagues. It was the Bangladesh cyclone appeal and it was in the early nineties, I think 1991.

As youngsters we followed the adults and did quite a number of fundraising initiatives to raise money for the Bangladesh cyclone appeal. I really enjoyed doing that. I felt that I was doing something good to help people affected by the cyclone, so that steered me into getting involved in numerous initiatives that saw me organising, facilitating, giving particularly around charitable endeavours.

I got involved in raising funds for the Royal Oldham Scanner Appeal.

I was invited to join the board that was created to raise money from the Asian community of Oldham and was led by Mr Iqbal Ahmed (Bhaisab). He is a very well-known entrepreneur and philanthropist in the Bangladeshi community. He managed to mobilise a team of people, made up of members of the Indian, Pakistani & Bangladeshi communities, to come together for such a worthy local cause. Can you imagine more than two decades ago a small community, merely 5% of the population, without the wealth that exists today, recognised the need for an MRI scanner? At such an early age, this group of people came to the frontline to support the NHS and the community at large and similarly, we note today, the Coronavirus pandemic has now brought people to the fore to support the NHS. At a young age I was involved in raising a lot of money for the Royal Oldham Scanner Appeal. I understand its relevance, to have an MRI scanner local, because my father had a brain tumour, and every time my father needed an MRI we had to go to North Manchester Hospital. There were times when we didn't have a car, so we had to take a taxi and that was quite costly. When I did have a car I was working, and so I had to try and get out of work to make sure that I supported my father in his visits to the hospital. I understood from personal experience what this appeal was all about and I got really involved, putting together a big programme, along with Mr Iqbal Ahmed and the team, to raise a contribution towards the £1 million that was needed. I was immensely privileged to be involved in this way and see the benefits of it afterwards.

Lottery Bids

As I noted previously, I was also involved in Oldham Bangladeshi Youth Association from 1991. I wrote a successful national lottery bid to get £120,000 for setting up an IT centre. The reason behind setting up an IT centre was that, around that time, maybe one or two people had a computer or IT facility in their own home. The vast majority of the youngsters would not have access to IT and I thought it would be a good idea to get some money to create an IT learning centre in the heart of the community. The lottery bid was submitted and awarded in 1996. This was very, very early in the days of the internet, of course. I recognised the need for an IT centre and I came up with an idea to put a bid in to the National Lottery, which had just come about a couple of years earlier, giving funds to community groups. I wrote the bid, wrote the concept and also did the costings. It was successful, so I was over the moon. I thought to myself, 'Wow! I raised a huge amount of funding by writing a bid and I was successful!' It was a huge amount - £120,000 in 1996 was a lot of money.

This was a 3-year funding project so a lot of it was capital cost, but I was really happy. I think word had spread across numerous towns that this group of young people had successfully attracted this amount of money, and people are asking me to write applications for them. I wrote another bid for a group in Tameside, in Hyde, called the Sylhet Tigers Club, who wanted to set up an education centre. I wrote another lottery bid for £200,000 which was successful. I was getting quite well known now for writing successful bids.

Then, in 1996, I pursued another application. I was working in the Single Regeneration programme, so I had access to data relating to health and well-being of the Bangladeshi population, and I recognised at the time that there was a lot of people who are dying as a result of coronary heart disease. There were a lot of alarming figures. As a result of that I spoke to another organisation - the Oldham Bangladeshi Association - which my father used to be the president of, but at that time it was Abdul Mannan, a very respected member of the community. I spoke to them and I said, "Look, the community is suffering from coronary heart disease, circulatory diseases. It might be worth putting an application into the National lottery for a healthy heart project. Your organisation is best placed to run this programme to raise awareness of coronary heart disease and provide prevention programmes to a community clearly not accessing the services relating to heart disease."

They were keen to do that, so I wrote another bid, and I conceptualised the project based on all the figures that I was seeing. I wrote the bid for £200,000 and that was awarded in 1998. Again, I was really, really excited because individually I could only help maybe a handful of people, but having an initiative and strategy would help hundreds. I thought this was another great way of me giving my ability. There's only so many things you can do on your own. If you had a strategy or an ambition and you created programmes, you could reach lot more people and it would be a lot more long-term as well. So, the healthy heart project was started and the idea was to support people with having a healthy lifestyle - healthy living, exercise, nutrition and dietary advice and guidance - and lots of different initiatives within that.

Oldham Central Mosque

After those three bids, I more or less stopped writing bids because I was getting busy with my work, I was married, I had other things to do, and I just took a back seat from writing bids and projects for other people. Although I stepped back, I recognised that there were other initiatives that needed to be supported, so I got involved with the Oldham Central Mosque. Not much happened in the 90s, but in the 2000s we finally managed to get the ball rolling with the fundraising and the construction of the project to build this really big mosque, a project for community worship and various other things - learning, funeral service and so many other things that are the heart of the community. Initially it was going to cost just over a million pounds but in the end the final cost was around two and half million, so I was heavily involved in the fundraising aspects of the project and gave my input to do quite a lot of fundraising - for example doing telethons on Bangla TV during Ramadan. As I had some media experience, it was an honour for me to brief everyone on how the telethon would work and how the telethon would need to be structured. I was in a team of highly capable people who made these telethons a success. In fact, on two occasions, my friend Robiul Khan suggested we do a power hour during the telethon which ended up raising a lot of money. I was supported by a telethon team which included the late Nijamul Islam and Anwarul Islam, among many.

I remember the first time we went I did a lot of the briefing to the committee and the volunteers that were involved about the do's and don'ts of going on TV. Sometimes I still look at those notes I made because of the knowledge I'd gained through a lot of involvement in the media. We raised more than £240,000 in one night. Year on year, we would raise a couple of hundred thousand and so on. We managed to raise the bulk of the money through the telethons over about 6-7 years.

In addition to that, I - along with committee members and volunteers - coordinated a number of other fundraising initiatives, like doing a 5km run in the community and a big dinner for over a thousand people. The great thing was I was able to call in a lot of volunteers, about seventy of them, to support this initiative and make this project a reality.

I was quite pleased and proud of this. The reason why I was so engrossed in this project is because I remember many years back, when I was quite young, my father stood up in the congregation during Eid prayers, at the Belgrade Hotel, and said, "You know what we need in Oldham is a central mosque", because at that time the prayers were held in a hotel lobby, a hotel ballroom. There was a time then, we used to go to a little mosque. I remember him standing up and saying, 'If you agree with me put your hand up', so all the congregation in the Eid prayer put their hands up and that's how the whole concept proceeded and the idea for the Oldham central mosque was founded. As well as doing good, it had a personal meaning to me to be thoroughly involved in it. Prior to the announcement he made at the Eid prayer, he had a big meeting in our house with his closest friends, committee members of the small mosque and together they decided that there was a need for a central mosque. My father being the president would make the announcement to the public to get their buy-in. Some of the key people at the meeting would have been the late Abdul Mannan, late Abdul Goni, late Abdul Zabbar, late Shomuz Miah, late Ataur Rahman, and few others whose names I struggle to recall now. These are the true founders of the mosque.

My father was quite ill so he couldn't be as involved in the latter stages, but when the first brick was laid they called him to do the laying, as the person who initiated and founded the concept of Oldham Central Mosque, many years previously. The project is complete now and thousands of people are benefiting from the mosque initiative. Whilst it does what it does as a mosque, it will increase some of its activities in the future by providing mental health help, counselling and things like that, and learning for men, women and children. Going into the future, it may develop a number of initiatives to support the community. Whether it's relating to education, economics, health and well-being, the mosque has the potential to not be just the place of worship, but a huge place for social change because of the nature of the amount of people that visit it – for instance, school visits have been happening recently. It's great to know that I've had a small input in making that happen.

The Arts and Charity Work

There was a time in the 90s - and then it kind of moved into the 2000s - when Bangladeshi arts and culture and heritage was a big thing and we grew up with a lot of Bangladeshi arts and culture. Even I myself was involved in literary initiatives and drama. We were using culture as a way to develop ourselves, and then at some point I recognised that the whole arts scene was dying, so I had a conversation with the arts council and we did a research project into the arts. It was called 'Inclusion, Involvement and Investment - Bangladeshi Heritage Communities and The Arts in the North-west of England' and it was funded by the arts council. It's quite a bit of a report, I have to say! I wrote the foreword. Culture is a very important thing that people should not lose; instead, they should take the positives to transform their lives. Culture has the ability to make a lasting difference to the identity of a person or a place. We now live in a diverse cultural landscape, that has become a rich mix of cultures which has benefitted me profoundly, and others should use culture as an opportunity for improving community life.

I did this project with another group because I felt that the arts and culture scene was dying in the 2000s – coming from being a very rich and cultural entity in 1990s. I wanted to identify what was going on and how we could bring together the artists that are still around and ensure that arts and culture and heritage scene didn't die. The report has a list of everything in there to ensure that at least some of the arts was sustained. I visit Bangladesh at least once a year, and during these visits I do learn about how culture is high on the agenda and how culture - including art, literature and music - is the beating heart of the country; its richness is very inspiring for me.

Because I had all these visits, I started seeing Bangladesh through the eyes of the English people that were going. I got involved with BRAC, which is the largest NGO in the world, and a big kind of charitable programme in Bangladesh started by Sir Fazle Hassan Abed, who was something of a role model for me. And so I had the opportunity to get involved with Vision Bangladesh initiative, thanks to the confidence of Penelope Mawson, which was a Sightsavers international - a BRAC joint initiative. Again, I mobilized a lot of people across England, worked with BRAC and raised a lot of money, for up to 100,000 cataract operations in the greater Sylhet region. It was a great privilege for me to work with many Bangladeshi people from across the whole of the UK to bring them together to support this initiative.

Often, what we do is we give £20 for a cataract operation. This initiative was a great idea because you are helping more like 100,000 people. And the more money that was collected, Sightsavers matched it. The total amount was, I think, around £2 million, 100,000 cataract operations - quite an achievement! I wanted to be a part of it rather than just constantly giving £20 or £40 for a cataract operation, depending on who was asking. I visited Bangladesh with some community leaders and the Guardian media group to witness the cataract operations, and it was great to see the donations coming to life.

So, we did that, and it was fantastic. Then I did the London marathon for the MS society, and the reason for doing the London marathon was because my wife has Multiple Sclerosis. I just thought, 'One day I am going to do this and I will do it because she has MS and it's close to me and it will raise some awareness within the Bangladesh and Asian community around Oldham and Greater Manchester and further afield, on social media, about what is MS.' It's not very easy to explain MS. In Bengali, just like with dementia, it is very hard to explain and often it is so difficult for people to fully grasp what MS is.

I also did a Manchester 10K for the Christie cancer hospital and after that I was invited to join the Maggie's cancer centre's board in Oldham. I did that, because again, I know people close to me who have had cancer and I know that, during their lifetime, one in two people will be touched by cancer. I thought it was very important for me to have involvement in cancer charities and support them, so that they can support the many people in our communities - regardless of which community they are from. This was something that needed further awareness and it was something that I felt that if this figure of one in two people in their lifetime will be touched by it is true, then who knows how many people it will touch in my family? Cancer does not discriminate, so it is important for me to support cancer charities, so that my contribution can benefit many people, people who I will never meet and never know, but I will know that I made my contribution to help them.

So, I wanted to be closely involved in that, and being involved in the Maggie's Cancer centre fundraising board. I had the privilege of being involved in many of the fundraising initiatives of the organisation and bringing in funds for the organisation as well as raising the profile of what it does. Maggie's has many fundraising projects, and ones close to my heart are the gala dinners, the culture crawl and the 500km cycle challenge.

The Singerkatch Probashi Health Centre

This leads me to one of the biggest initiatives in my life that I helped initiate: the building of a village health centre in the village where my family and I originated from - Singerkatch. Originally named the Singerkatch village clinic - now it's called Singerkatch Probashi Health Centre.

The idea started in 1999. It was after the visit to Bangladesh in 1998 where Liz Carney, a BBC Radio 4 producer, went with me. She was interviewing me and she saw me giving 500 taka to a number of people who approached me as we were walking along the dirt track road to the bazaar. She kept asking me, "How often do you give money?" I said, " Oh, every time I am here, I give money, I give 500 taka to every person that comes to me. The same people come to me every time I'm here, and I give them the same amount of money. Nothing changes for them; nothing changes for me either." So, she asked me, "Why don't you do something more sustainable? Why not create some sort of an employment project or something?"

I thought about it and, in 1999, I called a lot of young people of my age from my village who lived in Oldham and we had this discussion about how we should do something for the village as a gift to them, because our fathers and first generation had built the school and various other things, and they supported the village in many ways, but our age group hadn't actually done anything significant - and it had been like 30 years since we'd left.

So, we had this conversation amongst a group of ten of us and we basically narrowed it down to what we wanted to do. Different ideas were floated like, for instance, building something educational, employment related, and then we recognised that, where our village is, the nearest proper medical centre – or a clinic, hospital type place - was Sylhet. Sylhet was about thirty kilometres away, by the time anyone who was seriously or critically ill went there, they would probably die on the way. So, we thought we would try and do something relating to creating a medical centre.

In the year 2000, when we went back to Bangladesh, we did a consultation exercise and Radio 4 were with us again. They recorded it and they played it out on File on 4 as well. We had this village meeting and we asked these people to come up with ideas of what they thought was the biggest priority and most pressing. Similarly, they came up with the idea of a health centre, so I felt that was great that both us in Oldham and people over there felt that the medical centre was the greatest priority over everything that was required in that village. We started off this campaign at £10 a month from ten people, and we thought, 'we'll collect ten pounds a month and we'll only need a few thousand pounds to create something and that'll be it'.

But as time went by this £10 a month hardly grew. After three years it was still not enough. The whole thing carried on, and we were getting a bit demoralised, thinking, 'this will never happen'. One of our goals was not to ask people for money. Our idea was to generate that money among the ten of us, because charity becomes a dirty word when you ask too many times. We just thought 'we won't ask people we will just give it ourselves'. We gave our £10 a month, £10 a month... and there came a time when we were like, 'we're either going do something or not do something', because we were simply not collecting enough money. After a few years, it was a choice of: should we carry on doing it, or just call it a day and give everyone their money back? But people said, "We started this thing, we need to finish it" and what was just the seed of an idea then grew. We had some designs done of what the health centre would look like - costed it out and so on - and it became a big project; well over a £100,000.

Now we were thinking, 'How are we going to raise this money? Because we don't want to ask people, we wanted to be able to go to people and say, "We have enough money, we're just short of a bob or two, give us some money!" In the end we did a telethon and we raised about £40,000. Following the telethon, we did some dinners and we raised again substantial amounts of money. All of a sudden, we had all this money - now we could go ahead and build. So we had the designs done and land donated to us. Unfortunately, we couldn't get access to that first piece of land donated because the owners of the land before that wouldn't giving us road access, so it became very difficult for us. So many of us had gone from this country to create the foundation-laying ceremony; and we got there and we were not given access to the land before us. It was, to the say the least, rather unhelpful and very rubbish, basically. Village politics got in the way. We walked away from that and, within a day or so, one of our committee members, Azmoth Khan, and his brother, Ustar Khan, donated a piece of land that belonged to their mother and that land was given to build the new health centre which wasn't too far from where we originally planned to do it. We did the initial stone-laying ceremony and then the construction work started.

The project completed in 2016 and today, the health centre is up and running. It employs 7-8 staff, it's a primary care health centre in the village, it's got a doctor and various other staff. It does day surgery and things like that, and it is similar to a GP surgery. Everyone who is identified as poor is given a medical card and they come with their card, show their card and get free check-ups, get seen to and get three days of free medicine as well. The health centre sees anywhere between 300 to 400 people a week and the majority of them are women, with the majority of the people who come there displaying gastrointestinal issues. The more serious patients are referred or asked to go to the city - so this is more like a primary care facility. It's like a going to normal GP practice here though they are able to do minor surgeries as well.

In January 2020, I was part of a group of dentists that went to Bangladesh - I was supporting them - and we did a dental camp in the health centre. In the dental camp we saw about 300 people who had their teeth taken out or were given advice on dental care. So that was quite an achievement. My thing with the village health centre personally is that my dad did a lot for the village - built a school and so forth - and I wanted to get some of my age group to turn something into a gift to the village. It was quite an emotional thing that I, along with my colleagues, were able to do this, to benefit the poor.

We could continue to give money to people to have health-related check-ups and things, but it wouldn't have made a lasting difference - which is why we created this initiative. I hope it will grow as we are in talks with other providers to help it do so, for it to benefit more people and become more sustainable in the future. See more about that in Chapter 6!

The Importance of Giving

These are just some of the highlights of my giving, to give an understanding about what's in my head about giving. I also did a lot of fundraising for Mahdlo Youth Zone, a youth zone which is serving over 5000 young people in the borough of Oldham. 'M a h d l o' is 'Oldham' backwards. I did quite a lot of fundraising for them because I felt that young people were the future and that's why Mahdlo was established - it resonated with me. When I was younger, I didn't have many opportunities and didn't have much in the way of facilities to go and visit and take advantage of. I thought this was a great thing and I should contribute to it - so I was doing quite a lot of fundraising for them. I even attempted to do a half-marathon in Dhaka but that got scuppered because it was the day that the Islamic scholar, Delwar Hossain Sayeedi, was sentenced at the court and the country came to standstill. The following day was the half-marathon but I never managed to do it despite being there in Dhaka at the same time. It was just not possible.

In my hometown of Oldham, during the Rohingya refugee crisis - when the Rohingya people were being persecuted and they were moving towards Cox's Bazaar - there was an Oldham Rohingya appeal which was initiated by a young man called Moklis Miah (also known as Marcus) who got me involved, really just to be like an older head. In the end I was in charge of keeping the money. The whole Rohingya appeal became about sixteen different initiatives and these sixteen different initiatives created sixteen different programmes and activities. They all raised money from different activities, whether it was football or snooker or running, dinner events, cupcake sales - so many different events. Many women got involved, children got involved, and we raised just over £50,000 pounds with which we built the Oldham Rohingya village in one of their camps in Ukhiya. We paid for a hundred shelters which would house 800 people, we paid for packs for their shelters and we paid for water tankers. It was a great initiative once again to support persecuted people, and then we did the same again for Yemen. The Oldham Yemen Appeal did exactly the same thing and we raised just over to £30,000. The bulk of the money went to a large water tank that would provide water for thousands of people every day, and the rest of the money was for food and bread and things like that. Those two things were significant because it engaged whole groups of people – women and children as well as men - that hadn't happened in Oldham for a very long time. And in all of this, there's been the little things that I've done: like help people getting jobs, filling in forms; going to hospital to interpret; or just help consultants understand they were talking to an individual who had cancer and who was completely frightened; connecting people with services and making their lives better hopefully; supporting house building programmes for people, for poor people in Bangladesh, and so many other things.

Looking back over the decades, the importance of these bids and fundraisers and so on isn't necessarily on the legacy of how long they last. Sometimes, these things are only here for a short while, to do their purpose to help and then come to an end. The IT centre obviously helped a lot of people with their homework and things like that, with the homework club, but it changed after three years, and it didn't continue in the same way. The organisation continues and they have IT suites now, so one could say it continued but perhaps it didn't continue the way I wanted it to. The organisation still exists in a small kind of way, not the dynamic way it used to be – they do have IT facility and suites and they help people in a different environment, a different zone. The healthy heart project has gone though. It finished after three years. Just one of those things but it is a pity. I eventually stopped because I think people didn't have the right intentions or interest in running it in a way that could have led to it continuing now. It is more needed now than it was then. But other initiatives have come about to help people with the health and well-being - so something else continues in its place.

With the arts project, I just did the report to highlight to keep the arts alive. It does continue to be kept alive by various groups of people in various guises, but nothing quite strategic. Hopefully, an arts and heritage festival might pull some of this together and revive the arts scene again - poetry, photography, literature, music, food, fashion - all that stuff will be brought back in.

Other projects are still running. The health centre in the village is running - it's going to grow, with the new partnerships that are being talked about. The mosque is growing, new congregations are growing, more initiatives are being presented to the community. The scanner is being widely used in the hospital. So, a lot of these things do continue and I am quite grateful and privileged that I was part of seeing them come to fruition.

Depression

When it came to writing bids and fundraising this way, I never had to be trained what to do. It was an instinct. A lot of my things I've done have been done on instinct - the instinct being that I was confident in my ability to do something properly. If I wanted to go after something I would. It was like a spiritual pull that enabled me to go ahead and make things happen. Without a doubt, I believe that the blessings of Allah enabled me to do these things. However, in 1998 I was hit by a bout of depression which lasted for a year. I had lost a stone in weight because I was not eating properly, I was anxious all the time and my brain was working overtime. I just felt anxious and angry and afraid and scared and I couldn't sleep, couldn't eat. I was just in and out of my room all the time. I started smoking when I hadn't smoked before. I was just like going round, in a little bit of a merry-go-round. I wasn't sure what was happening to me. If I'd imagine pain in my chest, I would get pain in my chest. I'd imagine pain in my kidneys, and I get pain in the kidneys. And all these things happened and, when I went to the doctor, they said they couldn't find anything clinically wrong with me. This went on for a year. I struggled at work. I just couldn't concentrate and I secretly told my boss at the time, Nick Andrews, that I wasn't the same person.

Eventually I had to tell my Dad because he was witnessing the change in my behaviour, as parents do. I was sleeping in a separate room from my wife and daughter because, obviously I was up all night and I was disturbing them. So, I slept in the small room for six months and it was just a bizarre and very strange and a very scary time. The reason for having this bout of depression was because there were a few people that I was very heavily involved in and I used to trust with everything as I was growing up as part of the Oldham Bangladeshi Youth Association. I started finding out they were trying to discredit me to people in the council. They were trying to discredit my name in the council. They were talking behind my back and saying bad things to my friends. I just couldn't handle it because when you trust people wholeheartedly and when you believe in them, you think that they have helped you as well on the way. When this happens you find it really difficult to accept and I just couldn't accept - because I'd given so much of my time, my mind and my words in support of these people - that they would start doing that to me.

I got to the bottom of it because one of the assistant directors who went to Bangladesh with us, he called me in his office and he actually explained to me that a certain individual had been saying things about me and that I needed to be very careful around these people even though I thought they were my best friends. Similarly, another individual did the same with another director who - although he didn't tell me directly, he told my best friend Kashif Ashraf- told for me to be careful around these people.

All of these things drove me mad. I just couldn't figure out what I had done wrong. I hadn't done anything to them and all I could figure out in the end was that these people didn't like other people climbing the ladder. They wanted to hold them back by discrediting them. A whole year went by and I had younger members telling me, "We will tell you things that you should never repeat because we will not be able to come and defend it, but these are things you've been vilified by X, Y and Z". I just couldn't figure out why, because I haven't done anything to anyone. All I am doing is trying to help people. But I think the overarching comment that I used to hear was that, because I was trying to climb the ladder and I was doing things - writing bids, helping people set up projects, taking these trips to Bangladesh, creating a bridge between Bangladesh and Britain and professional people across the border - connecting people and making things happen, some people didn't like that; so they would do all these things behind my back, to cause a nuisance for me basically. Which they did - they caused me depression and I suffered a lot. During this time my whole family suffered with me, but, thanks to the prayers of my mother, father, wife and the support of some new-found friends, I was able to shake off the depression.

At that point I decided that I didn't want to climb the ladder anymore. I just wanted to be where I am, I just wanted to be happy. I'd only been married a few years and I had a daughter. I didn't want to feel like this in the future. Unfortunately, they continue to do this, but it's not as bad as it was before. I am able to navigate it now, hence my idea of giving more. Keep giving, keep giving, keep helping people, because you will get their blessings. In addition to getting their blessings, you will get people who will talk positively of you and will help you to navigate the journey of life in a very positive way. I must say, very clearly, that if you ever become a victim of depression, do seek help immediately and don't suffer in silence.

The Belief of Giving

The reason why this is a chapter about my goals in giving - which is almost parallel to my daily life, my day job and things like that - is because I totally believe that if I give, whatever that may be - whether it's a smile, whether it's a pound, whether it's a million pounds, or whether it is organising something - I absolutely believe that by giving I will receive in a miraculous way. Obviously in Islam we believe that if you give you will get a return of more than what you give, and your wealth doesn't diminish. Now, that's the wealth side of things, but as an individual I wanted to make sure that I was on hand to support anyone that needed support in whatever way I could. And people would constantly ring me, always talk to me, phone me, come to see me and I would be happy to support them in whatever endeavours they needed support with, or even just get information - I would give them the information so that they could make better choices.

So yes, I believe, completely and utterly, that people who give will receive in so many different ways, and in more than one way. Some receive a return on their giving if they gave money - I am sure that a lot of people become wealthier, and they don't become poor by giving up their time and so forth; as Muslims we believe Allah will increase wealth and not decrease it. And people will talk positively of you; whenever my contracts have finished in a job, I have always walked into another job because not only have I always believed I have the ability and capability to walk into a job, but also at the same time I believe that because of doing good, someone must have thought good of me and someone, somewhere along the way will have put a good word for me if I'm going for something new. Not only that, I believe that your Rizq – opportunity - is guaranteed and no one can take it away. It comes by the will of Allah - but make sure you work hard for it.

It's always been like that. I never felt that in all the times I've given I have not seen the rewards. The connections I've made that have led to work here and there, just knowing the right people in the right places, opening doors in places that I could not have even imagined. I always used to say to a brother-in-law of mine - who is a very wealthy, millionaire kind of character - he always used to say to me, "Money is everything, money is everything, money is everything". I used to say to say to him, "Money isn't everything, money isn't everything, money isn't everything!" I used to say to him, "I can open doors that your money can't." He never used to believe me, but I think these days he does. He does understand the value of knowing the right people in the right places, just for knowing sake. You don't want anything from them, and they respect you more for that. If you know people and they know that you don't want anything and they know you're not a parasite who only wants to know them because of their knowledge or their money or something that they've got, they respect you. If you're a parasite then people generally don't remember you kindly and they don't want anything to do with you after the first few meetings or want to get to know you. There is value in giving, because it says a lot about you in the eyes of other people.

Whereas I am the opposite when I meet people. I really don't want anything of them, but I do want to understand how they got to where they are, because it gives me great amount of satisfaction being able to narrate that story to somebody else who is trying to achieve something. To say, "Well I know these people - this is how they've done what they've done, what they have achieved, and if that's what you want to do than that is how you need to push ahead". But you need to understand one thing: it's not about take, take, take. It's about give, give, give. Hence, the more you give the more you'll get. If you're all 'take, take, take', all you're doing is hoarding, and that hoarding doesn't get you anywhere. You might have a big bank balance, you might have a big house, you might have big car, you might have a lot of big material things, but in the long run it doesn't create your legacy. It's not something that that will satisfy you later on because, when you die, what will happen to all your wealth? You're not going take it with you!

My father was a classic example of giving. As a result of his giving, ten years later, his name is still talked about every single day. I always say that he is one person where there's not a single day that goes by when somebody is not talking to me about him. Every day, for the last ten years, every day I get somebody saying, "Your dad was a very kind man and very helpful to me". He is forever alive, his name, his aura is still here; which enables me to keep going in a small way. I'm not as great as he, but in my own way I just keep going, knowing that he is a rich man. He is gone but is a very rich man in the sense that he is well remembered, he is well liked and people always reference him when they are talking about important moments - whether it is the new mosque or the new community centre, or the amount of people, in the voucher days, that he had helped to bring to Britain, to make their lives better and their extended family's lives better, to the thousands of people's forms he'd filled in over the years at the advice centre. I try and live by some of those values so that I feel satisfied in my heart that I have given what my purpose is - hence I have this tagline called, 'Serving My Purpose'. I created that line after questioning myself: What is my purpose? I realised this: to serve is your purpose, wherever you are. So, by serving your purpose I am serving my purpose. I want to really run this idea of serving your purpose - of giving and getting manifoldly in

return as the whole thread of what I'm trying to explore here in this book.

Chapter Five:
Cycle Tour

Planning Another Trip

The highlight of all the trips to Bangladesh I organised was the cycle tour from Sylhet to Cox's bazar, where we successfully raised awareness about climate change and its impact on the country. You might well ask, how does cycling raise awareness of that? What made us decide to cycle at all?

The simple answer is: we wanted to cycle! After visiting Bangladesh so many times, we needed a good reason to go again, other than just visiting family. We'd done all the different types of trips we could do - education, sports, music, arts - and it was almost like, 'Well we need a reason to go back, what else do we need to do there?' And I'd had enough by then, taking all these people and having all the headache and losing my hair over it!

Having said all that, I thoroughly enjoyed the adrenaline of cycling and because Phil was a cyclist all his life - as a police constable when he first started on his bike, and also being a keen cyclist - we'd started going out on the bikes, just to lose weight. Before that, I'd not been a keen cycle enthusiast and thanks to doing that with Phil, the idea developed then into, 'Why don't we just take the bikes and cycle around the country? Because if we're going to the countryside, there's hardly any vehicles and it will be such a great summer holiday kind of feeling, on our bikes and into the villages.'

I was just imagining my village, roaming around there and into the neighbouring villages. Just on our bikes with all the paddy fields on the side, clean, green and fresh air everywhere, blue skies - memorable and romantic sceneries. That's what I'd imagined the cycling trip would look like, though it ended up being quite an organised international, 50-60 miles a day kind of deal. An enjoyable road trip but in a different kind of way.

The idea behind this venture was that Bangladesh was going to be amongst the top ten countries, if not number one, which will be affected by climate change. Sea levels rising causing people displacement, water borne diseases, food shortages, are amongst the many events predicted to happen soon and the evidence is there that many of these already occur.

The first thought was simply that we just wanted to do a cycle tour. We knew we wanted to cycle from Sylhet to Cox's bazar but we didn't know what such a journey would look like. We just drew a line on the map and said we want to go from 'here' to 'there', initialling planning to go from the top of the country, the mid-north, to Cox's Bazaar, but that would have taken twice as long and we didn't know the terrain or the route. We didn't know anything about that area and I didn't want to put ourselves out. Instead, we started at Sylhet because we knew it well. It's great to be there because you get the right kind of welcome and everybody knows the ins and outs of the infrastructure. We knew it was the right place to start.

Then we thought, 'Well, we need to attach some theme to this; some beneficial theme other than us enjoying the ride. What can we do that would be globally acceptable in Bangladesh?' We came up with the thought that climate change, at the time, was being highlighted in various media forums and at Bangladesh government level because Bangladesh will be so affected by climate change that it was a relevant topic to highlight amongst people in rural areas.

Mr Asad Alam Siam, the Assistant High Commissioner at The Assistant High Commission in Manchester, said they were very keen for us to go and promote Bangladesh in a positive light. They were very helpful in getting the visa sorted for us, without even asking any questions, and they were very welcoming, to the point that they invited me and Phil Buckley to go have tea with the High Commissioner to talk about what we were doing. Obviously that explanation was also partly due diligence for them without asking formally what we were going to do, but they had confidence in what we wanted to do and what we had done in the past. They were happy to support us and gave us a letter with all our riders' names on to keep with us just in case the local police or local officials wanted to know what we were doing, in addition to them having already written to the foreign office for them to circulate our details through the various departments. They gave me a letter with all our names saying, 'These are the people who were going to go to Bangladesh for the purpose of cycling and promoting Bangladesh and we welcome them to do that'. Basically, everyone had to carry that letter just in case anyone got into trouble, it was a passport to show who we are and what we were doing.

The other great help was Mr Mohammed Salauddin, who was the general manager for Biman Bangladesh Airlines. He used to be the country manager in Malaysia but before that he was the manager of the Manchester office of Biman. He was very keen for us to fly Biman, for us to experience Biman. If we were going to Bangladesh to promote Bangladesh, then we should not go Emirates, we should fly Biman, and so we did. They took our bikes and everything and it was fantastic.

The bikes were all our own and we took them from the UK, boxing them up into cycle boxes and taking them on the normal luggage. 20 kgs of bike and 20 kg of clothing, that was it. Despite simply being boxed up in cardboard, they made it one piece and we just assembled them at the other end – hard, though some readers might find, to believe!

The Team

Our team were made up of mixed men and women, mixed Bengalis and white, one black person, and included a team doctor. It was a very good mixture of people. The trip would not have happened at all if it wasn't for Jebi Raman, at the time working for BRAC UK office, and we crossed paths during an event organised by Iqbal Ahmed in Manchester. When she said she worked for BRAC, I was very keen to learn more. She was working on a project called Parishad, which meant her plan was to get young Bangladeshi graduates or professionals from England to volunteer for BRAC in Dhaka and elsewhere. When I mentioned to her that I undertake a lot of trips to Bangladesh, and I was going to do this cycling trip, she was very keen and subsequently we had a number of conversations on the phone. I think she said, "If you do this trip, I'd really like to come along and help you organise it."

At that point I thought, 'I actually could do this'. Otherwise, I'd have shelved the idea, because me and Phil, whilst we had done many trips together, there was still some apprehension about taking on this unknown territory. Then Jebi said, "Yes I can get BRAC involved and we can support it. I'd really like to do this." Now, I must add here, Jebi Rahman was working for BRAC UK at the time, and she saw an article about the proposed bike ride in a newsletter published by Asian Tigers Capital. She was the one who convinced me and motivated me to make the cycle tour a reality; so I owe Jebi my gratitude for giving me courage and being by my side all the way.

Then there were later conversations, like my sister and brother-in-law, who wanted to go. Another relative on their side, Zilla, wanted to go also and a friend Naomi, who was from Outer Hebrides!

So, there was a whole group of them and I thought, 'This is great! I've already got half the group in one family and it shouldn't be difficult to get the other half amongst my circle.' I got a few people along, and then gathered more. When I used to work in Leeds I was doing a goal-setting training course and there was this guy called Omari Williams. He came to this training session and I'd never seen him before but just mentioned to him that I was going to do a cycling tour of Bangladesh. How it's all about goal-setting and we're setting this goal now and we're 'gonna make it happen', etc. I just mentioned this to him and he said, "I'd love to come." I said "Really?" and he said, " Yeah, let me go home and talk to my partner." Within 24 hours he said, "I'm coming, what do I need to do?"

Omari is a very sporty person, who has a masters in sports science and currently is a football agent for a number of football players. So, he has really gone up in the world, along with being a part-time lecturer at a university. Omari came along on the trip, a keen footballer, a keen martial artist – and so we had to make use of our local people - the guys that often went out with me, including Phil.

And so we gathered them all together - cyclists from Scotland, Naomi, Mathew, Jelina; London, Jebi & Zillur; Sheffield, Omari Williams; Greater Manchester, Anjub, Aminur, Jahangir, Dr Musharaf Hussain and Phil Buckley too - giving us a good mixture of seasoned cyclists and novices. So, we had a group! All this time it was me and Phil doing what we know how to do, there was Clemon, our sponsors, doing some stuff on the ground and there was BRAC, who also sent a person to do a risk assessment because Jebi and her family and friends were raising funds for Vision Bangladesh - the project about doing the cataract operations mentioned in the previous chapter. They were doing some of this fundraising as part of our cycle ride, as a charitable thing as well. It was also interesting to note that Matthew Berlow, Jelina's husband, had never been to Bangladesh after his marriage so it would have been new for him; and Jebi's best friend, Naomi, had never been at all - so that was a great time for them to go. Jelina had just had a kidney transplant, so it was important for Jebi to take her sister, she said to me it, 'I want to take my sister to Bangladesh, she feels happy with her husband and this will be a great opportunity to go and be a group' - and that's what we did. I am very grateful to Jebi for keeping my thinking in the right place.

The Cycle Tour

Believing the tour would be a good idea, I decided to speak to our sponsors in Bangladesh - the Akij group – and they were keen to be part of this adventure.

The history of Akij Group stretches back to latter part of the forties. In its infancy, the group started in quite a humble way with jute trading. Jute is known as the golden fibre of the country, and in those days was earning the highest amount of foreign exchange. The founder of Akij Group is the late SK Akij Uddin whose inspiring story of hard work, vision, bravery has been passed on to his five sons. Together they have taken the industrialist & philanthropic family business to the highest level of enterprise in Bangladesh.

I became good friends with the middle brother of the five, Sk Jamil Uddin, when we became acquainted on a previous trip. We took Oldham

Athletic Football Club for friendlies in Bangladesh – the first British league side to go. He had just started off in the family business which owned this brand called Clemon and I got to meet him then. Then I just made a speculative phone call to him, mentioning to him that we will be coming to Bangladesh, but this time trying to do this cycling programme from Sylhet to Cox's bazar. We don't even know what it looks like, we said, no one's ever done it before, and Bangladesh hasn't had an international bike ride of that calibre. Would you like to be involved? Initially he said yes, maybe with like 5% interest. Then later he said, "Yes we can do this. Yes, X, Y and Z for you". I was delighted and said, "Yeah, X, Y and Z sounds good - if you can just support us, that will be just fine."

Then, every few days he'd message me saying, "Sorry, I've been speaking to the marketing department and we are going to do this, this and this". And every few days the marketing department kept coming up with more - ramping up the idea, making it bigger and bigger and bigger, until they created this entire programme which, essentially, I was really happy with because that just meant all the risks were mitigated and taken over by Clemon.

They would put seventeen members of their staff on the job during the seven-day ride and they would communicate with all the local authorities, the mayor's offices, the police, the ministries and get all the relevant permissions and road traffic management where it was needed - sort out everything in-country which made my job easier, and meant that we just had to turn up and do it. They even helped us organise places to stay. I must admit some places were pretty shambolic but other places were really nice! You get that with the experience of doing something like this. And that's how Clemon came to be involved. They took it all very seriously because it was also an opportunity for Clemon to come out in a big way into the country's advertising scene. Jamil did say to me, "You are bringing foreigners to Bangladesh. It is our duty to make sure they have a good time and go back and talk about their positive experience, creating a good image of the beauty of Bangladesh."

The team were fantastic. Without them it wouldn't have been the same programme. I think we would have just gone and done a cycling tour and come back, and that would have been it. We wouldn't have the interest of all the television channels, the members of parliament, mayors, heads of police, other dignitaries and things like that in every division that we cycled through, not forgetting the hundreds of cycling enthusiasts that joined us every day along the route. The Akij group had also organised a group of cyclists from an organisation called Kewkradong to join us for the whole tour, and they were also joined by other cycling enthusiasts - to name a

few; Bangladesh cycle tourist Syed, Mazharul Islam Tareq, Homaed Ishaq
Moon, Robiul Khan Mona, Muntasir Mamun Imran, Muzakkir, Sharif,
Faisal, Mahbub, Delwar Hera, and Sumon. The tour campaign aimed to
promote two benefits to cycling:

    a. It improves your health and well-being,

    b. It's a mode of transport that doesn't give out fumes into the
atmosphere causing pollution.

That was it. That would be the campaign, to get more people to use
responsible modes of transport. Although in Bangladesh a lot of people do
use bikes already, we knew this tour could be used to promote this healthy
form of transport through television, radio, billboards, newspaper articles
and stories, so we thought that would be a good idea.

Then Clemon came up with the idea of a band. They have their own
band, a rock band, and they came up with the idea that every night where
we stopped there would be a band show. And we would then be on stage
talking about the impact, and also what climate change is, what should people do to be much more aware, alert and try to play their part in mitigating
it, as well keeping an eye on it for the future. That was the whole idea, and
that's what we did. Every night there would be a concert, every night we
would speak into microphones, the director of Clemon would speak, and
myself and Phil Buckley would then speak about climate change. Every
night we would speak in front of between anywhere between 5000 to
15,000 people. Generally, they came for the rock show rather than wanting to hear about climate change, but it was a captive audience and all the
television channels carried the same story. So, the ride then became 'The
Clemon Ride for Green' as opposed to just us cycling from Sylhet to Cox's
bazar.

The Road to Cox's Bazaar

For a lot of people, the thought of cycling the roads of Bangladesh is
not a good one! The roads are known for often being full of holes or being little more than rubble and sand. But when we cycled from Sylhet to
Moulivbazar, and Moulvibazar to Brahmanbaria, the roads were brand
new and smooth. From Brahmanbaria to Comilla, to be fair, the road was
not very decent - at least one stretch of it anyway and then the rest of it
was good. Surprisingly the main highways were very good. Chittagong to
Cox's Bazaar, Chittagong to Chakaria (all new tarmac) and Chakaria to
Cox's bazaar. On the last day, the road was like brand new tarmac - made
for cycling! It was clear the government was investing in road infrastructure, as the economy was growing.

Along the way, we had to be careful and wary of potential dangers. We were paranoid about drinking the water, for instance as the last thing you want on a tour like a cycling tour is to get 'The Belly'. The last thing you want is any kind of illness when you are on that kind of tour. Can you imagine if one person was ill? You can't leave that person behind, can you? What would I do as the guide? The organiser has to be with them, go to hospital with them - a whole different story would open up if somebody fell ill. Thankfully, everyone took the right precautions and all were well but it was a constant worry.

With that thought in mind, I would also like to say that this tour would not have been possible to manage without the immense support of Dr Musharaf Hussain, who not only was the team doctor but also provided great leadership on the tour, as I frequently found myself too busy with operational matters and feeling overwhelmed and tired every day. Dr Hussain was a godsend as he took up the leadership role as needed and he commanded a lot more respect from the group than I, being an older and wiser head!

The chosen ending for our journey, Cox's Bazaar, was partly because none of us had ever been there before and on the map it looked all downhill, although it wasn't! Cox's Bazaar is obviously a very famous place, so it was just one of those arbitrary decisions, we will start from Sylhet and finish off on the beach in Cox's Bazaar. We'd jump in the water and that would be our chance to go and see this famous place, something we've never seen before.

I think the fact it was the first time was also the pull for a lot of people. Out of everyone who went with us, none had ever been, so that kind of pulled in people thinking, 'Yeah I would like to go see Cox's Bazaar, I've heard so much about it, so much photography and footage, let's see what it's all about.' And it was great! We'd never done anything outside of Sylhet other than being in Dhaka so everything was brand new to us and, given that Clemon would look after everything from security to the risk assessments, we were very comfortable. So we said, 'Let's do it!' Clemon were great, after all, for advertising purposes, it would have been easier for us to do something in Dhaka over a seven-day period, because that's where all the publicity is - everything happens in Dhaka. But they let us finish in Cox's Bazaar and I'm very glad they did.

It took seven days to ride from Sylhet to Cox's Bazaar and, to be honest, when we cycled in we were really relieved we had finished. Then everyone lay their bikes to the side and jumped into the sea. A few minutes later four or five of them carried me and took me into the water because as the team leader they were really happy that I managed to get them through safely, and so they picked me up and dumped me into the water!

It was a really fantastic feeling. Cox's Bazaar, being such a nice place, is always in the back of the mind, and the reality didn't disappoint. Although later on, the following day, when we were looking around, I thought the developments and infrastructure could have been a bit more organised. But, given where it was, it was still good. We stayed in a nice hotel and we had a barbecue tent at night. We went to visit a waterfall and everybody was dancing around a campfire on the beach. It was all surreal, like being in a movie for that evening. A huge tent was lit with fairy lights - it was like an entire tent was made out of lights with a campfire in the middle and the buffet station. Everybody was there.

Next to the tent was a 20-foot movie screen which was showing the film '2012' to an audience on the beach, all in aid of us. The big stage was set up to give everybody a medal, 60 people recived one on the beach. It was like a dream, an amazing atmosphere. I'm very grateful to Clemon for organising all that. Then we went following day to see a waterfall and we drank lot of coconut water. We played beach cricket on a second beach. We went to Laboni then we went on to Inani. Inani, in 2010, was not inhabited at all, it was really empty back then, though I think it has developed further now. The beach there is so clean and beautiful and a good development of infrastructure would make it as prosperous as anywhere in the world.

Everything ran so smoothly with the tour but the only difficulty arrived on the way back. The Biman officials at the airport - not all of them, just two or three of them - gave us a lot of grief trying to get the bikes on the plane because they kept saying, "The diameter is too big, you have to pay extra excess for the extra diameter. If you don't, you're not going to take these bikes." I had a banging headache, the people who were with me, they were in shock, and everybody was saying, "No, we're not paying excess because we brought these bikes, we're taking these bikes and we've got the letter. We got one of the Biman officials helping us on this trip - how is it possible that some Biman officials on the counter are giving us this grief, demanding extra money for the excess diameter?"

That went on for hours. In the end I tried to get Mohammad Salauddin to phone from Manchester to the airport desk to tell them who we were and that they should not cause us difficulty. The bike packs had gone in the Biman hall on the way in, so they had to go back on the way out. But they didn't listen to him either and, in the end, I just told everybody I am just going to pay them because otherwise they're not going to let us go and we're going to miss the flight. It was a little disappointing that this happened right at the end, but this is what happens sometimes.

The Draw of Bangladesh

I was born in Bangladesh and, of course, have a Bangladeshi passport, but I also have a British one too and so we do have dual nationality. My family, having lived the bulk of our years here in the UK, see ourselves more as British and less as Bangladeshi. My generation is in between these two states but my children's generation will be identifying themselves as British, whose heritage happens to be Bangla, whose heritage is Islam - that way around. We could say British Bangladeshi – Banglaspeaking Brits!

With that said, 'why go back to Bangladesh?' is a question which can be asked. Many people might find they had a heritage in a different country and culture but wouldn't necessarily feel an urge to go there. Why do I go back to my land of birth? I go partly because I've still got a few relatives alive, so that's one of my sincere reasons for going. Another really important part is that my early memories keep calling me back to the village. The third reason is this: every time I land there, I feel I have come home, even though I do perhaps two weeks and then I am ready to come back!

It's like I need a booster injection. I have to go once a year, twice a year, three times a year, just to get that booster. It makes me feel like I am on a happy pill, I go and I come back happy, and a few months later I am ready to go again. There is a really strange thing going on inside me which I am sure many other people experience at the same time, but it is incredible. As soon as I land in Dhaka, I take a deep breath and I think, 'Ahh, feels good; it feels good to be back'. It feels like you're home - you're excited, and you get in the car, going past the roads and the shops and the smell and the sounds and it's like, 'Oh this is so great!' You get to the village and you're walking along the dirt track, you're walking along the river, walking to your auntie's house and everybody is saying hello to you and you're saying hello back to them. These people are folks you've seen since you were six years old and they are still the same. Only they've grown older - and so have you! Then there's the other kids who've grown up since you left and don't know who you are, and they are thinking, 'Oh, who is this who has come to our area?'

It's always beautiful to visit the bazaar and just mingle with people you've known for years. A lot of people have left, a lot of new people have come up, and people are always intrigued because my father built the school and everybody knows whose son it is who's arrived. You get respect from people and you want to be around them; you want to support them and be a part of what goes on. I just get engrossed in it. I feel at home, and there's a lot of good reasons why I should, but at the same time I feel like coming back after a few weeks. I've never stayed more than two weeks and I always say to my wife that at some point soon - health and well-being being right - we ought to go and spend the winter months in Bangladesh – three to four months - see how it feels and, if we like it, we ought to go occasionally - it may happen!

Chapter Six:
Building the Village Clinic

An Idea is Born

In 1998, we went on an education trip to Bangladesh as a follow-up to the trip in 1996. During that visit we had a journalist from BBC Radio Four's programme, 'File on Four', who was following a group of teachers for a programme called 'The Ties that Bind' - meaning the ties that bind the pupils of the school with the places they come from in Sylhet. While this journalist was in our company, she also followed me around in addition to the teachers, to see what I was doing. One thing I had arranged was a meeting in the village to find out what I could do to support the village. The Journalist saw me giving out money to people as we walked along the road, which was essentially a dirt track, and she was asking what I could do that would more substainable. I was like, "yeah a that's good point - I will go back and think about it"

Upon my return to Britain, I arranged a meeting with a few people of my age group, young people who were very close to me from the village, who lived in the UK and had grown up there. I had this conversation with them, "Let's do something for the village, let's give them a gift." No other infrastructure had been built by British Bangladeshis who had been involved in doing things in the past, like building schools and supporting poor people. Over several meetings in 1999, we came up with the idea, that we needed to set up an organisation to improve the lives of people in poverty, perhaps through a number of development programmes. We acknowledged that the first generation had built schools and madrassas, including many other projects that have supported individuals when they needed support - whether in healthcare, education, marriages, or building bridges - supporting them in any way really. But since then, a gap of thirty years passed without any significant infrastructure in the village.

We discussed numerous ideas, ranging from improving education, or some kind of economic project, to even founding a healthcare facility. But then it dawned on us that there was no proper medical facility, the only thing that was available in the local bazaar was a number of pharmacies that used to prescribe medication to people. There wasn't really any MBBS qualified – Bachelor's of Medicine and Surgery – doctors on hand, it was really just what the pharmacists provided. Now you can imagine how, without a proper qualified doctor in the village, people would frequent these small pharmacies to recieve medication based on what the pharmacist has prescribed, and hope that they would be cured. People would also turn to herbalists and spiritualists for healing, which meant that the health of the villagers was very much a hit-and-miss affair really.

So we thought, 'Yeah let's try and create a medical facility.' We didn't know what it would look like so, in the embryonic stage, over a number of meetings held in Oldham, ten people came forward to become the founders of the Singerkach Development Committee. We developed the constitution, set up a bank account and a chairman was appointed, Mr. Habibur Rahman. (Sadly he has passed away at a young age, and he is very much missed by us all for the passion and graft he had towards creating and sustaining this project.) I was secretary and a man called Abdul Ali was appointed treasurer. Then it was agreed that we would raise funds, but first we needed to give £10 a month ourselves to create a fund base, before we could go and ask people for money. Our goal was not to ask people for money until we were self-sufficient and had enough of our own budget, we would only ask people for money if we felt that we were stuck. This idea of creating your own fund base came from my late father.

Meeting the Village Elders

After that trip in 1998, we returned to Bangladesh in 2000 with Radio Four, this time for a programme called 'Cementing the Ties'. They would follow me half of the way and then follow the teachers for the other half. We had a consultation meeting in the village, discussing numerous ideas, and the village verdict, delivered by the headmaster of Singerkach High school, disclosed that they wanted a medical facility. The village elders gave their verdict that a medical facility was needed because the nearest one was in Sylhet, about thirty kilometres away, meaning that people travelling there would have to be able to afford it. When people are in severe or critical conditions, it is difficult for them to travel that far. For many people this means they don't get the right treatment which leads to more serious illness, or death, on the way.

The work of village elders is very important. Singerkach is made out of a number of little villages within the whole, called paras. I don't know how many there are exactly, but these paras make up the entire Singerkach village. We have a number of post offices and schools, the infrastructure that serves the entirety of that village, and one bazaar. Then, in each para, you'll have one, or a couple, para leader(s) - like the elders. When a decision needs to be made at a village level, they'll all come together and meet on the grounds of the school or similar, and talk about wider issues relating to the whole village. A sort of a village council.

In order to do anything, whether you're in the village and you want to do a project similar to ours, or you're an outsider going in and wanting do something else, it is absolutely essential to consult the village council. If you don't consult them, if you don't have their buy-in, if you don't take their views on board, you won't, regardless of how much money you have, be able to go in and do it. I know people who are very wealthy from this village, living in various parts of the UK, who try other approaches, but they've failed because they thought that with lots of money they could go and buy a piece of land and do something with it. They've not managed to do it because they didn't have the support of the whole village, we were very lucky to have been able to get them on-board, listen to their views and deliver them, and we've not had any major issues – other than some other people trying to cause difficulties along the way.

You don't just get to be a village elder; you must have some common sense. You have to have fairness and rationale and naturally, as you develop and become an older person, your integrity, your honesty, and your fairness shine and people look to you to be the one that needs to be an elder. That said, if you have a bigger family than the rest of the people in the para, your elders are going to be the chief - that's the other way it works. Sometimes it's about might.

There's no kind of formal swearing-in, but this is a kind of informal process that people will agree to once a village elder has died. The villagers ask themselves who should be the next person we look up to; who should be the captain. Generally, they will pick somebody, but it doesn't have to be a strict process with many different hurdles. It may just be like 'okay' and even if the elder is symbolic, then just out of respect they'll say 'okay this next person', even though they may not entirely be the whole package. They might just do it out of respect. Also, some of the people underneath the main elder person act like the engine, running the show.

I know in my para our village elder is one of my cousins, Mr Sharif Khan. He used to live in England but he settled back many years ago, so it is widely accepted that he has a global view on matters, he has integrity, stature, he supports the poor, building houses and water pumps, people go to him for advice, he holds court in his village house and has various other charitable endeavours. A natural elder.

The Planning Begins

Having received the confirmation of the village elders, we embarked on this project properly and undertook some further research. For example, in the year 2000, I visited numerous NGO-run health centres and clinics in Sylhet. We visited Marie Stopes, the Ragib Rabeya Foundation and an NGO outside Dhaka run by BRAC which was, I think, in Narshingdi. We visited a model health centre run by BRAC and spoke to the doctors; we talked to Marie Stopes and the Ragib Rabeya Foundation to understand how these three different models worked, and what they did.

You might well ask, why didn't we partner with these NGOs? Firstly, we wanted to do it independently. Secondly, Sylheti villages - a large number of them anyway – often have links to people who live in the UK, or the Middle East, or similar. So they have a channel for generating income that comes back into the village, and in turn these villages aren't usually in a dire state as other parts of the country are where there aren't many people who are economic migrants elsewhere, sending remittances back to enhance and develop lives of those they left behind. We didn't feel the need then to call upon an NGO at the time. Visiting these places though, taught us a great deal.

It was a learning exercise to understand how the in-country facility would work, getting into the village, and what type of things we could provide, as well as the expertise and resources we needed. Once done, I came back with what we'd learned and informed the committee. We carried on just giving this £10 a month and meeting every so often, but this went on for years and I think that at some point we got frustrated because it appeared as if it was never going to happen. £10 a month was not going to get us there.

Only ten people meant it was a hundred pounds a month, which wasn't really going anywhere. After a few years, I think we were all losing interest. Some people were saying, "let's have the money returned to people; let's call it a day, it's not working." But others said, "no we started this, we need to carry on." And so, after about eight to ten years of working like this, we decided that we needed to go out and fundraise to a wider audience. We had several meetings to get support from wider groups of people in places like Birmingham and Oldham. We organised a telethon on Channel I Europe and raised quite a bit of money! We also held some fundraising events - dinners and sports events - and finally we managed to get all the money together to start building the facility.

We went to Bangladesh to register the land, that was donated by a mother of one of the trustees, but we couldn't get access to the land because the previous owners didn't want to give us access from the road. This was basically out of jealousy, 'we aren't gonna assist them' kind of thing. Even though we would have paid for the little strip that we needed to take the road, they were being difficult. In the end, luckily, one of our trustees, along with his brother and their mother, generously donated a piece of land which was opposite this particular one, and gave us roadside access.

Building a Health Clinic

We wanted to do something to mark our land and make a big thing of it, so we had a ground-breaking ceremony to celebrate the beginning of the work. We got shovels and we dug into the land and we had a prayer, a big meeting, a big stage setup and a big audience. We explained to the audience what we were doing. Doctors from England and doctors from Sylhet were with us, and it was an opportunity to formally tell the village that this is happening. We had a blessing ceremony and once that was done, the land was blessed and it was ready for the drilling to start.

We did the ground-breaking ceremony and then started the work. We had a lot of consultation meetings in Oldham and Birmingham, and we also talked to people from the village who had resided in various parts of UK - London, Swansea, Milton Keynes, Humberside and other towns - explaining the vision to them and trying to get them interested. So many people came on board. We also organised a conference in Oldham, invited people from the village, and kept informing and presenting the case for the need for this health centre, more importantly doing something to save the lives of the severely poor and needy. We had drawings and video footage to show what it would all look like. It was just an opportunity to consult, but also get a buy-in from people who would eventually become donors and support the programme.

We had an initial design done by a local architect in Oldham, but that was eventually changed because it was too big for the project. Eventually another drawing was produced by an architect from the Sylhet municipality, which was much smaller and maybe more affordable for us. Initially our budget was quite high and then we scaled it down to about a quarter of that budget. In the end, upon completion, it cost us about £140,000 to just build the facility – which consisted of two floors with quite a bit of land left, to do what we need to do in the future.

It would be great to pretend we did all the construction work ourselves after the ground-breaking ceremony but, of course, we didn't. We hired local firms to do the work. The drilling was done by a company from Sylhet town. First they had to test the soil, which they did by digging in - perhaps about 50 feet down - to ensure that all was proper. It was quite deep. They took the soil out and checked if the soil was good enough, or how much of the piling, or what kind of piling, they needed to do, because building on a paddy field is not exactly a normal piece of land! The field was about eight foot below the road, so it would have been waterlogged a lot during monsoon season. We needed to ensure what the soil was like. In the end, obviously, it was fine. But even though it was fine we didn't take any chances because we needed to do proper piling. When we were making the base it was quite expensive, but it needed to be done just in case we faced problems and the building sloped like the leaning tower of Pisa!

It is easy to sound like an expert now – all this talk of 'piling' and 'soil testing,' - but, in truth, I didn't know any of that when we began. I read about it and spoke to various people, picking things up from them. As we went along, we managed to create a picture of some of the things that needed to be done. Thankfully, we had people around us who had built houses or mosques, or school's and were able to advise us. Then, from what I know through reading or my brief understanding of some of the processes that construction can go through, I was able to imagine the picture of what needed doing. Then obviously we had to ask our advisor - who owns a construction company in the UK - and an architect – the municipality architect from Sylhet – to guide us through it in Bangladesh.

We also had support from a number of doctors in Sylhet, particularly Mahmudul Majid Shaheen, who was well-established and well-reputed. He liked what we were doing and was very happy to see that sincerity, honesty and a genuine desire to support poor people with their well-being motivated us. He came on board and helped us with purchasing equipment, layout and signage, appointing doctors, and various other things so it looked like we were setting up a health centre, and not a restaurant or something. We needed that expertise and so we got it! Along the way we also had the guidance and support from Dr Musharaf Hussain, who was general practitioner in Rochdale; and Monchab Ali who, at the time, was a chair of the national Bangladesh community organisation, Greater Sylhet Council UK.

We opened the facility in 2016 and ever since, we've appointed various people – doctors, nurses and other support staff. It's just like a general practice drop-in facility, like a primary care, and sometimes we can do day surgery depending on what it is that the patient needs. We've got some daycare rooms where people can go. There are beds, in case they need a saline injection intravenously; that can be done along with stitching. If they need an ECG for heart testing, that can be done too. Just the basic things that need to be done, more serious cases obviously have to go to a bigger, better facility in town.

On record, the centre sees up to around 400 people a month, mostly women come, plus a few men and some children. They come with the usual typical symptoms. They come with gastrointestinal issues - around a quarter of the patients complain of this, possibly to do with the high spice diet and the high level of stress that causes acidity to form. It's all working fine and, currently, the wages and the bills are funded by the people who donate the £10 a month. Some people are now donating £100 a month and £50 a month, and there's a regular donor list of up to thirty people - entirely funded from the UK. We are hopeful that we are going to go into partnership with a number of other charitable health-care providers and organisations. We are going to go into a partnership with them so the centre can be sustained, and it can grow to see and benefit more people.

One of the next stages is to create a diagnostic facility with ultrasound, endoscopy and full x-ray machines. Also, a maternity unit is urgently needed, so that deliveries can be done by qualified nurses in a safe environment. This is because we are aware that over the decades many young women have died in childbirth due to complications of home delivery, complications created by infections. Having a maternity unit would ensure that babies are delivered safely, and women don't die in labour through infections.

Overcoming Difficulties and Future Plans

I guess deep down there were many difficulties we faced. None of the committee members who established this project had any medical background. It was all people who ran take-aways, restaurants, and some of us worked in professional jobs, but no one with a medical background. It was very difficult to do anything other than give the headline that we're building a health centre, to help people with healthcare. Nobody really knew anything about what needed to happen, we had to gauge the support of these medical experts in Sylhet that, thankfully, came on board and gave us the support, otherwise it would have been very difficult indeed.

The dream was to develop an alliance with the British Bangladesh Medical Association, or the various hospitals in the UK, to create a twinning, but that didn't happen because - at every step of the way - while it was exciting, it was also kind of tiring and personally I lost focus. It wasn't happening and I wasn't pushing it as much as I should have been. Luckily some of the other members took up the baton when I was feeling down and didn't want to do anything about it. Some of the other guys stepped up and when they used to accuse me of not doing anything, I used to say to them, "Actually you know what? I am glad you say that, because sometimes you can't rely on one person. Everybody else needs to chip in somehow. I am just really grateful that you are empowered enough, and you have the motivation enough to pick it up when I lost interest or when I don't feel like doing anything. That means that there is more than one person who can take this thing forward in the absence of one not feeling right or not want to do something. This project will go forward."

We also had to encounter a lot of criticism, particularly from people who were villagers who lived in this country, who, through sheer jealousy, didn't want to take part in what we were doing but wanted to criticise it a lot, telling other people not to donate because they weren't leading the project themselves. They didn't want it to happen and they would go out of their way to make sure they put up barriers and closed doors, things like that. We used to hear all these comments via third party sources, from the ones who had had that information whispered to them. We had to deal with a lot of the politics - politics, with a small P - from our very own people who should have been supporting it. For me, that was especially frustrating when young people are trying to do something positive for humanity. I viewed this sometimes with anger, and other times with thinking how low people will stoop, how pathetic they can be.

When you do certain good work, a lot of people automatically assume that you're doing it because you want to make a name for yourself, or it's not really a genuine cause, or they question where the accountability for the money is placed. The first thing is that people have a criteria of whether they agree or disagree with you, and if they disagree they will find every single criticism under the roof to be able to condemn the initiative with. We weren't immune to that. We faced a lot of that from our very own people, whereas people who were not from the village but were from elsewhere and whose origins were perhaps from villages in different parts of Sylhet, they were more excited - "Wow! These guys are doing something for poor people in their own village! This is great, this is amazing. We need to understand how they are doing it."

It inspired a lot of people externally, but internally we faced the same problem in the village as well. There was a whole group of people that supported and wanted it, as they knew it was a need. And then there was a whole group of people that didn't want it to happen. Again, they would put up barriers and they would spread negative whispers, and so we had to overcome quite a lot of that over there as well. Thankfully our organisation and our people in the Singerkach development committee all held the same vision, were all on the same path, and we couldn't be distracted. We didn't have in-fighting, that's why we stayed together for over twenty years.

We've even had interference from politicians in Oldham, who perhaps wanted to dictate certain things that we did or didn't do. I would not have it. I had very strong disagreements with some of my committee members, who were influenced by some of these local politicians about who should and who shouldn't be involved during the fundraising. I didn't want to play that game. My view was that we were doing this for the sake of Allah and for poor people. We were doing this for humanity, and we were doing this so that we get the reward in the life after because we believe in that as Muslims. I was not standing for anybody who wanted to interfere and play games and we faced quite a lot of this kind of behaviour but overcame it. Thankfully the project is carrying on and we hope that it'll go into the next stage via these alliances and partnerships that we are looking to develop.

Developing the project is very important. Many people have built similar projects to our health centre, but even if they manage to keep them going, it's not just the infrastructure, the building itself or land that keeps the project alive, it's maintaining and training the staff, and sometimes staff just move on. Buildings that were originally health clinics end up turning into nursery schools because it's easier to get someone to do things that kids need. The project collapses and the building ends up being used for something else. The continuous needs for finances, is a difficult task to maintain.

Getting a doctor in a village is difficult because all the doctors want to work in the towns. Luckily, we got one who comes in everyday, taking about an hour to travel. We had a female doctor, and we've got others - they call them 'half' doctors - and other staff such as nurses and support staff. We've managed to keep them because we pay them good! We also give free treatment and medicines to the poorest people. Anyone who hasn't got a medical card - which entitles them to free treatment – gets charged a visit fee - it is really nominal considering that if they go to the nearest place, Biswanath or Sylhet, they will be charged around 500 taka (£5) per visit whereas we charge about 30 Taka (30 pence) per visit for people. So, we generate a little bit of income like that, and also sell medicines. This way we're managing to keep it going. That is just nominal levels. We need to scale, and in order to do this we need to have alliances and partnerships. I am very hopeful that we will continue and that some of the other people coming over to help will take over the management side of things. If we get management and the funding side sorted out, it will be fantastic.

A question I have been asked since the start of this project is, will I now build something else? A school perhaps? The answer is: no, I don't think we need to do a school. We have a number of kindergartens in the area, as well as a government-run primary school, secondary school and college. The secondary school now has college status, so it is a really great development for the area. I've not really thought about what else would be of interest for me to do - other than that, my biggest interest at the moment is climate change, ever since the bike ride in 2010. Although, I would be interested in running personal development programmes to inspire, motivate and facilitate change within the community of young people in the village and beyond. I believe this would help them in their journey to sustainability.

In 2013, I went to Istanbul in Turkey to take part in the global climate reality leadership programme run by the Vice President of the USA at the time, Al Gore. Gore created the climate reality project and I did the course over a four-day period during the time when the Taksim Square riots were taking place. That was quite scary! I went there and there were about 600 people that came from 70 different countries, and we all went through this leadership programme. I became a member of Climate Reality as a climate change leader for them and I would go back and do a number of talks occasionally as a result of this.

My biggest interest now – simmering away inside of me – lies in my village and centres around the issues of climate change and how it affects the people of Bangladesh. If there was something that I would do next, if I had the ability, time and resources, it would be to do with climate change, because flooding in the country is taking its toll. I've seen images of our village house and the water is very close to the veranda. If it rises by another foot, it'll flood the ground floor. Despite being landlocked, Sylhet is affected by flooding. I think the reason why is that typically a lot of the rivers have been silted up. The riverbeds have risen, and in some of the culverts people have taken them over and built on them.

Lots of big ponds have been used for developing housing estates, so there is nowhere for the water to be held any longer. No basins anywhere, just dramatically reduced and shrunken areas. That's why riverbeds are much higher up and the rivers are not as ferocious as I remember when I was a child; the little culverts have all been taken over. They no longer look like culverts, they look like land with houses and things on – roads, etc – and a lot of people's ponds are not ponds anymore. They're not deep enough and have been covered with earth to build on, there is nothing to hold the water. An additional problem is that there's talk about India controlling the water flow and, when it gets too much water, the authorities open the dams and the excess water then comes in to Sylhet and other parts of the country.

The problem here is that people's day-to-day concerns are about livelihoods. I can go in there saying, "In ten years' time, in twenty years' time, in thirty years' time, your children are not going to have anything, if climate change takes its course. They're not going have land to live on", and I am sure people will laugh at me and reply, "well our concern now is about our livelihood, about food. We'll cross this bridge when we get to it." The question is, how do I craft this idea and will I be able to get people to understand it, believe it, accept it and start taking action? If I can overcome that hurdle, then I could do something relating to climate change and that would be beneficial longer term - not just a quick-fix. I have to find a way I can say to people that we need to think about this issue now - let's plan ahead for your children, and the ones going to be born, coming into this world. That might bear fruit but again it's a long-haul thing. I would have to spend a lot of time out there. It would be an entire movement of things that need to be done, it just can't be done sparingly. You can't just throw money at it because it just isn't going to work, it has to be an ideological change. We will have to see if, one day, I can do anything about this.

Recently, Bangladesh was declared as no longer being a developing country. After thirty years of doing tours and visiting commonly, I can say I noticed the changes physically. I can see through all my visits I've done and I've seen it through the eyes of white British people and professional people that have gone - from the very first visits to the last, there's been huge development. Without a doubt the industry has taken a lot of people from various villages and put them into jobs, given them a wage and given them a livelihood that will be going back to the villages - like Bangladeshis in the middle East, Europe and America are giving remittances. Similarly, the workers that are coming to the factories are feeding taka back to the villages.

The standard of living has definitely improved, but the problem with these improvements is that the problems also increase, they don't decrease. The need and the demand for different things appear and the population increase has been massive. If the increase hadn't been so huge then the improvements would probably have been greater. Even so, with the increase in earnings and increase in standards, reduction in beggars and poor people, and lot of physical infrastructure improvements, things have certainly changed. There's a lot of localised work available in the service and manufacturing industry, and all you have to do is buzz around that time and you can see that everybody is going somewhere. It's not like they're going somewhere idly; they are doing something somewhere. Even a little kid on the streets selling eggs can sell those eggs, take the money and buy some food for the family. Everyone's enterprising, they're doing something.

Home and Away

In the last chapter, I said that my family and I see ourselves as British, but how do the Singerkach people see me? I can say that they see me as a bideshi, a foreigner! That's not necessarily how I see myself, of course.

When I get there, I feel like I belong there. A strong sense. But I think the generation that knew me as a young boy has passed on, and those of my age group have gone to the Middle East or come to Britain or gone elsewhere. Anyone who sees me now, when I hear them talking, when I am walking past people, somebody will stop and say, "Who's that bideshi? Who's that foreigner?"

That might seem strange, after all, I look Bangladeshi, I talk the language, I'm part of the culture. It's not like I'm a white guy coming to visit. How can they tell? It's what you wear, how you wear it, how you talk, how you stand, what's your posture like - everything about you. The locals can smell you a mile off! I don't mind, I'm cool with it all. But it is interesting to think of how others view me.

Many British Bangladeshis can easily become cynical of those from their villages back home, because they are seen as bideshis, and rich ones at that. I can understand that. They have every right to feel so because a lot of them have probably been short-changed, in more ways than one, when they've come to visit. My approach to Bangladesh and the village life is this: when you go over, don't show off because you've done all right. There's a lot of people out there who are just making ends meet, so there is no need to go and start flashing the cash, and talking and acting beyond your status. There is no need for all that. You need to find a middle ground where you respect where people are and also show yourself some respect about how fortunate you have been, having the opportunity to go somewhere and be an economic migrant, working to make a better living, build a better house or eat better. But when you get to the village, not everybody is like that, not everybody appreciates that.

You have to be honest with yourself. You have to represent or present yourself in a way that doesn't make people feel small. I think people often forget that and they'll go and behave in a certain way which aggravates something and then they will get taken advantage of. I have been lucky, that's never happened to me. Partly because my father has a good reputation in the village for what he has done for people, so there is an element of protection for me there, and secondly, I don't go there and pretend I am someone I'm not. I don't go and belittle people. I don't go and interfere. I don't do things that will irritate people or offend. I stay well clear of those kinds of circumstances and situations, and my contribution to conversation and movement is based on smiling at people and giving them my salaam and asking them how they are. If somebody does ask me for a few quid, I give them a few quid, but I keep it at arm's length. If I didn't, I reckon sooner or later I'll fall into that trap of becoming cynical. People give me back what I give them. It really is true, this thing about giving and getting - you get what you give!

Late Asira Bibi (my dearest Naniji) with my cousin Abdul Basit (Ashraf)

A community meeting at Bangladesh Cultural Centre. My late father Mabaswir Khan (speaking)

Villiage home

Nani's Bari (maternal grandmother's house)

My father's first passport photo   My mother's first passport photo

Beautiful village scene

My sister, neice, cousin and aunt on a stroll in the village

Bahadur Khan

Fufu (dad's sister)

Nani's grave

Outside the village mosque with older cousins

Cataract patient at Vision Bangladesh – one of many projects I supported

Planning Meeting for Olham Central Mosque

My father laying the first brick for Oldham Central Masjid

Interview with **Mr Khan**

Background to Bangladeshi Independence War

In 1947 the British withdrew from India. The two independent nations of Pakistan, which was predominately Muslim, and included modern Bangladesh, and India, which was largely Hindu, were created. In this partition East Bengal, where most of the jute was produced, became part of East Pakistan and West Bengal where the jute processing factories were located, became part of India. The two provinces of the new Pakistan nation had almost nothing in common other than the shared Islamic faith. East Pakistan was separated by more than 1600 km from West Pakistan, and, with more than half the population of the new nation, it felt underrepresented in a government dominated by West Pakistan. In the election of December 7th 1970, East Pakistan's Awami League, under Sheikh Mujibur Rahman, won the majority of seats in the Pakistan National Assembly but was denied power by delays in the opening of the assembly This marked the beginning of civil war On March 26th 1971 East Pakistan proclaimed its independence as the new state of Bangladesh The national government of Pakistan responded by invading the eastern province.

The Pakistani army was eventually driven back, with assistance from India before the end of 1971 and Sheikh Mujibur Rahman became the first Prime Minister
The Macmillan Encyclopedia

came to England in December 1970, just after the general election. There was a lot of civil unrest at the time in East Pakistan. My family were living in a village in Sylhet in the East. We were listening to the news every day here in England, and on the 25th March 1971 the Pakistani Army started killing people. They burned house after house, village after village and committed many atrocities.

There was one village called Seramshi, near where my family lived, where a massacre took place and many women were dishonoured. The army behaved like animals.

There were about 64,000 villages in East Pakistan at that time. My relatives were safe, away from the fighting, but my nephew was in the Liberation Army (Freedom Fighters). They arrested his father first and took him to the police station in a village called Singar-Kach. But my nephew came and said he had nothing to do with it and he was taken himself Luckily he survived. Communications were broken at this time and we had no information about our family for about six months directly

Here in England, I was involved in a major campaign to raise world opinion about what was going on. On the first of August 1971 we had a huge rally in Hyde Park, coaches went down from Oldham and there were masses of Bangladeshi people from all over the country there. A petition was handed in to Prime Minister Wilson asking Bangladesh to be recognised as an independent sovereign state. The first country to recognise it was Bhutan, followed by India. We also were collecting money locally to send to the Freedom Fighters. We created a special fund. Here in England, relations between the Bangladeshi and Pakistani communities became very tense.

I was at home when the war finished. I had been in hospital having a gallstone operation and watched the news on television every day The Pakistani army surrendered and the 16th December 1971 was victory day. Sheikh Mujibur Rahman had been in prison in West Pakistan. He was brought to Dhaka and hundreds of people went to the airport to greet him. I watched this on the television. He looked very lean and thin. We celebrated here in England, and continue to celebrate on the 16th December ever since.

I think I will stay here because of my family ties. Three of my children were born here. I will try and write my life story to pass on to them in the future.

Mr Khan

Mr Khan, about the liberation war.

My first school, St. Hilda's

My wedding registry day, Liverpool, 1995

With my wife on our honeymoon in 1995

My father with his friend Geoff Philpotts,
at an Anti-racism campaign in Oldham

Leaders from the ethnic minority communtires of Oldham meeting.
An MP, Mayor and Chief of Police at Civic Centre

Me with friends in the 80s

With Sir Fazle Hasan Abed, founder of BRAC at a Fundraising event organised for Vision Bangladeshesh

Cycle Sylhet

Regular cycle practice with Phil Buckley QPM

Manchester 10k Run

The National Muslim Service of Remembrance (NMSR) 2021 at the Muslim Heritage Centre, Manchester

Festival of Light Oldham 2021

Ready to attend an engagement representing the lord lieutenant of Greater Manchester 2022

At the beach in Cox's Bazar at the end of Clemon Ride for Green

My sister's mehndi with family members

Honouring Abdul Mannan

THE OLDHAM ADVERTISER, THURSDAY, 21 APRIL, 2011

Our father would be so proud of charity set up in his honour

by Ruhubia Akbor

A LEGACY left by a community leader is set to continue with a new charity set up by his children.

The Amana Foundation has been launched in memory of Mabaswir Khan – a pillar in the local Bangladeshi community.

The founding member and former president of Oldham Bangladeshi Association dedicated his life to helping others and now his children are hoping to do the same.

Daughter Shamsun Khatun said: "We want this foundation to help those who cannot help themselves.

"We also want to introduce volunteering opportunities for children and young people and convey the message of doing good in the community, so they understand the purpose of giving back at an early age, just like my dad did with us.

"It is an ambitious programme, but I sincerely believe we have the talent, knowledge, skills and passion to take forward the values of Amana Foundation and implement the projects to continue my father's legacy."

Mr Khan first came to Oldham in 1963 after emigrating to England a year earlier. He worked in various local mills before returning to his native Bangladesh in 1966.

The teacher founded the Singerkach Public High School in 1970 before making a permanent move to Oldham with his young family in 1971.

Alongside other respected Bangladeshi community leaders the father-of-five was instrumental in forming a local action committee to help the liberation efforts in his native land. The committee later became the Oldham Bangladeshi Association (OBA) for which Mr Khan held the post of president between 1978 and 1991. He was also a leading light in the development of the Oldham Jamia Mosque on Middleton Road, Westwood and the Oldham Central Masjid and Islamic Centre.

The 75-year-old died last November after suffering a brain tumour.

The Amana Foundation was officially launched at the Grand Venue in Westwood on Tuesday.

Mr Khan's son Muzahid said: "We felt we had to do this because he dedicated his life to improving the lives of other people. We didn't want to lose that legacy.

"We are trying to instill his values into the next generation and give them some focus.

"My father would have been very pleased that he could inspire so many people to come forward to do good in society."

COMMUNITY STALWART... Mabaswir Khan, of Oldham. A charity foundation has been set up in his honour by his children

My father in The Oldham Advertiser

Amana Foundation honours work of community pioneer

LAUNCH: Coronation street actress Shobna Gulati attended the launch of the foundation in Oldham

Young members of an Oldham family launched a charitable foundation in memory of one of the town's community pioneers, Mabaswir Khan.

The Khan family launched Amana Foundation at the Grand Venue in Westwood last night.

Event

The foundation has been created by children, young people and women from Mr Khan's family to tackle the root cause of poverty and empower the local community both in the UK and Bangladesh.

Several volunteers, as young as four-years-old, have been actively raising awareness about the foundation and the community launch event.

During the evening children and young people performed poetry, literary reading, nasheeds and a short video was shown about the life and work of Mr Khan.

Surprise guest, Corona-tion Street's Shobna Gulati came along to help raise money and present certificates to the youngsters who helped to organise the event.

Activities for all the family including face painting, henna, raffles, photo studio whilst stalls sold jewellery, cakes, food, t-shirts and handbags to raise money.

The evening ended with a raffle draw and an auction.

Mr Khan's daughter, Shamsun Khatun said:

"We want this foundation to help those who cannot help themselves, we also want to introduce volunteering opportunities for children and young people and and convey the message of doing good in the community so people understand the purpose of giving back at an early age, just like my dad did with us.

Instrumental

"It is an ambitious programme, but I sincerely believe we have the talent, knowledge, skills and passion to take forward the values of Amana Foundation and implement the projects. Currently, over 43 local businesses and organisation's have signed up and pledged their support towards the foundation and that list is forever growing this is a very positive sign!"

Mr Khan dedicated his entire life to helping the people of Oldham. He was instrumental in opening the Westwood and Coldhurst Advice Centre serving thousands of Bangladeshi people who were in need of important services including, welfare benefits advice and help with immigration, housing, employment, racial issues and other problems associated with a newly migrated community setting up home in Oldham.

He was also one of the founders of the Oldham Bangladesh Association and the Oldham Jamia Mosque on Middleton Road.

He laid the first brick for Oldham Central Masjid and Islamic Centre in April last year.

Mr Khan died last November, aged 75.

Newspaper feature of Amana Foundation

Amana Foundation launch

Shobna Gulati with my mum and sister

Shofiqur Rahman Choudhury MP

Family in Bangladesh

Shonf Khan, Azam Khan and me

My daughter, nephew and neice

Volunteers of Amana foundation

Mohsin

My father looking content

Relatives in Mymensinghtown

My Uncles

Press conference for Clemon Ride for Green

My father with the Mayor of Oldham, High Commissioner of Bangladesh and
Chief of Police at the opening of the first Bangladesh cultural centre in Oldham

Centre moves to new premises

WESTWOOD residents now have a bigger and better advice centre to help in their everyday lives.

The Westwood Advice Centre has moved to new premises in Featherstall Road North.

Centre managers, who have operated in the area for 18 years, wanted to move from their old building in Main Road which was in bad repair.

The centre serves around 6,000 residents and offers advice on a range of issues including welfare benefits, immigration, housing, health and employment.

Pictured at the official opening are (from the left) centre manager Mr Mabaswir Khan, the then Mayor of Oldham, Councillor Margaret Riley, who was taking part in one of her final engagements before handing over her chain of office on Wednesday, and Mr Abdul Mannan of the Oldham Bangladesh Association.

16th November 2010

Dear Muzahid Khan

I was saddened to hear that your father had passed away He was an inspirational community Leader who I and colleagues had a great deal of respect for

It was his drive and determination that brought about the building of the Millennium Centre. Your community have a debt of gratitude to all the efforts Mr Khan devoted to the work of the Bangladeshi Association.

You and your family are in our thoughts and prayers.

Yours sincerely

John B Battye DL, FIBMS

Letter from John B Battye DL, FIBMS

HOUSE OF COMMONS

LONDON SW1A 0AA

All replies.
Oldham Office
11 Church Lane
Oldham OL1 3AN

Tel-0161 626 5779

24 November 2010

Dear Mrs Khan and family,

I was extremely upset to hear of the death of your husband. Mr Khan was an outstanding leader of the Bangladeshi community in Oldham and I value greatly the support he gave over so many years. He was able to give me an insight into how his community worked and how problems could be addressed.

His work in establishing both the Community Centre and Advice Centre was appreciated by everyone and the number of people he assisted over the years must be in their thousands.

He was always so very kind and helpful to myself, from giving advice to allowing me to use his home for meetings. He will be greatly missed by his family and his community I will personally treasure his memory and send my sincere condolences to all his family

Kind regards,

The Rt Hon Michael Meacher MP
Oldham West & Royton
Including Chadderton & Hollinwood

Letter from the Rt Hon Michael Meacher

Opening of the health centre

Phil Buckley QPM unveiling the health centre name

My father, son and nephew

Me speaking

The Singerkach Health Clinic

Ground breaking ceremony of Singerkach Health Centre

Me with Bahadur Khan

With my fufu

Photo of Biswanath police station

Delivering a workshop

EVENING CHRONICLE, OLDHAM, MONDAY, JUNE 1, 1998 —— 15

Voluntary worker meets the Queen

A WESTWOOD voluntary worker was meeting the Queen and the Duke of Edinburgh today in recognition of his services to the community.

Muzahid Khan (28), of Main Road, received an award to mark his achievements at a Buckingham Palace reception.

He has been involved with Oldham Bangladeshi Youth Association, Peshkar Theatre Company and the Royal Oldham MR Scanner Appeal, just to mention a few.

Progress

Muzahid, pictured with his invitation from the Queen, said: "I have had the opportunity to work with some very special people and I feel this recognition is not only for me but also for the different teams and individuals. I still don't know who nominated me.

"Voluntary work has helped me to gain skills enabling me to progress in my career."

Muzahid, who is married with one daughter, is employed by Oldham Council as a projects officer for the Westwood Single Regeneration Budget team.

At Queen's Garden Party 2022

Chapter Seven:
Family

My Parents

Family is an understated word. It is very important, and I wanted to stress how in this chapter. Why are your parents important? Because your mother and father are the ones who bring you into this world and they care for you until you are able to stand on your own two feet. They don't stop there, they carry on caring for you, blessing you and being there for you until they are gone. Therefore, it is essential to make sure your mother and father get the best of your love, affection and care throughout their lifetime, otherwise you are only losing the blessings and you can only blame yourself. Clearly, I was fortunate to have my father, who was a huge influence because he was larger than life and particularly because his entire life was devoted to serving people in order to make their lives better; whether it be through education, guidance and practical support. He became an iconic figure in Oldham for all the work he did to improve the lives of people. My father was devoted to helping everyone in the community, his devotion was a shining example of service to community.

My mother had to be very strong to be able to support that, but she was also the one who brought us up while he was busy being the President of the Oldham Bangladeshi Association, the Mutawalli of the Oldham Jamia Mosque, and senior information and advice worker at Westwood and Coldhurst Advice & Information Centre, helping people both during office hours and in his spare time. He had a total devotion to helping others. Every waking moment of his life would be devoted to that, which is why he is really remembered fondly, by people both here and abroad, even ten years after his demise.

I have so much respect for both of my parents. My father had a brain tumour towards the end of his career, and this would end up causing so many difficulties. After he retired, he slowly became increasingly frail. I had the good fortune of spending at least the last fifteen years of his life being there for him whenever he needed me - taking him to the mosque in the car, or taking him to the doctor, or the hospital. I'd be there in a flash to ensure that I was on hand to be his aid.

I got a lot of fulfilment out of being there for him in those latter stages. I probably would have had regrets if I hadn't because, in the early years when I was growing up, I was sort of being either a teenage-type character, or somebody who wanted to play football and be with friends all day long, come home, eat and go to bed. Later on in life, I realised I needed to do this for him, and in those moments, especially when we had journeys in the car from A to B, every time we were in the car, he'd always give me a piece of wisdom. For fifteen years he'd tell me things in the car that I didn't know, or give me certain wisdom that benefits me now. He'd always say to me, "Drive slowly!" or when I would be praying he'd say, "Why haven't you got a cap on?" or he'd tell me things about Bangladesh, people and their characteristics - a lot of things that I probably wouldn't have learnt if we hadn't had those moments in the car.

I believe that I am the most fortunate of all the siblings, to receive such wisdom from him, and that's great. On top of that, he was a very generous man. He gave all his time and money away for the benefit of people. He could have been a very wealthy man. I remember in our conversations he used to say a lot of his friends in the 70s and 80s were opening restaurants. They wanted him to be a partner. Some of his friends, those who were not literate, used to say to him, "Become a partner, Mr Khan. You can be the guy who reads the bills and sorts out the paperwork while we run the business and you can have a quarter share or something." He could have been a quarter shareholder of at least seven or eight restaurants, but he chose not to. He chose to help them anyway but didn't want any remuneration from them. Perhaps he just wanted their blessings, which he is getting right now.

I have grasped some of that from him. Had he gone down that route, he'd have become a very wealthy person. However, his purpose was to serve people, to support people and to make their lives better. He didn't want the trappings of this world, he wanted to prepare his life according to the belief of Muslims who believe in the eternal life, Judgement Day. He wanted to be more prepared for that in this world, which is why he never was interested in worldly trappings – cars, land, thing like that. Some of that belief system has fashioned the way I think as well. Although there's parts of me that thinks, 'I need to do this, I need to do that, or I need to have a go at being a businessman', I do think sometimes that I totally get why my father did the things that he did. I appreciate his philosophy now more than ever.

When I was younger I used to think, 'why did my father not take over the opportunities to become a good businessman? We could be so financially wealthy.' But spending that time with him, in those fifteen years, and now looking back on his life's journey, I think he did the right thing because his legacy is so big, his respect level amongst the community is so pure. If he had been very wealthy and if all the people that talked well of him did so because he gave them money, I don't think that would have worked at all. The love and affection he has left behind, given what he has done, he is getting back in return through genuine sincere love. I get it now and that has affected us as a family because people give us that love and affection wherever we go, because of the fact that he did it without wanting anything back. People remember that. Even people who have passed on, their children talk about him as well which is a nice thing left behind for us to remember him by. It is a nice blessing. I have total respect for all the people who loved my father, continue to remember him in their prayers, and always remind us of his valuable contribution. They tell us the likes of him will never come again in our community. Whilst I appreciate their words, I do believe that it is important for me to remember a few people who also gave lifetime contributions to society, like the late Shomu Miah, Maksud Ali, Abdul Mannan, and Abdul Zabbar. These were true leaders of this community; they were the giants on whose shoulders the community was built on.

My mother, on the other hand, I guess is the backbone of the house. Bringing five kids up and looking after the domestic affairs of the family is not easy. She spent her entire life in the house, rarely going out, and if you speak to her you would probably find out some of the difficulties and ups and downs of being in a foreign country which has now become home. In the early days, when we suffered a lot of racism, she came through it all. She is much stronger now - she was very apprehensive in the past - I would say very strong. She understands a lot of things because she has seen the issues my father has dealt with over the years, either within the family or outside. She is able to rationalize things and she sees things through different lens'. I feel like she is quite content at the moment, although she does worry still, even though her kids are now adults and married with kids. She still worries about us - that's a mother's love for you!

I'm deeply grateful to my parents for giving me the space to be who I am, space to do things even when they disagreed on certain things. They still let me carry on and, to be honest, I am really grateful that I have not turned out a bad person; and none of my brothers and sisters have turned out as bad people either. I guess parents have to instill those values into children in a certain kind of way for them to be who they are.

Siblings and family in general

I have two brothers and two sisters. Again, they are very genuine and gentle people, they go about their daily lives doing their things and everyone comes together in my mum's house during Ramadan as well as throughout the year. Every day, during Ramadan, we spend breaking the fast at my mum's because I believe that our mother deserves all the children to be around her during that time. Other than during the recent lockdown, we have never missed a single Ramadan. The lockdown was the first time in the history of the family we have not managed to eat in my mum's house, all of us together. But as far as I can remember everybody would always be at the parents' house and we all spend the whole of Ramadan together - which is quite unique and I'm very fortunate because there's many people around the world who would not be able to do that. I find that to be very spiritually uplifting and fortunate that we are all able to do that in one go.

That's why I think people don't often value family as much as they value friends or business acquaintances - because of selfish reasons. I believe that more people should value family because, without us all being there for one another, we wouldn't be as rich in our thinking and our interactions if we became seperate. We're much richer and much better for it. You do your own thing, but you still retain a stronger level of connectivity, communication and interactions, and you are there whenever each one needs you. Whoever needs assistance, someone is always there on hand to be supportive. Whether its financial, or babysitting, you know you've got your own ecosystem and that makes for good relationships with family members and siblings.

I know many families whose relationships have broken down, and that's partly to do with money, partly to do with people having got married. Different personalities have entered the family and different people have got different expectations. Misunderstandings take place and suddenly the family is broken up into pieces and people start going their own way. They can't stand one another and there's so much heartache. The parents are sat there thinking, 'we brought these kids up, what's happened here? How are they broken?' It causes depression, mental illnesses and it causes a lot of anguish, and it shouldn't. People should always build their lives on a certain set of values in relation to family. They need to draw lines that cannot be crossed. Lines based on values.

My Immediate Family

My immediate family is my parents, brothers and sisters, and of course, now I have my own family, that is, my wife and kids. When I got married, I felt like I married the best person in the world! I knew I wanted to get marriedthe first time I came across her. I saw values in her I admired. When you love someone, it is said that, you should love them for the sake of Allah.

I was completely besotted by her, her mannerisms and her values. I knew straight away there was no need to waste time, but to create the pathway to a proposal that needed to be sent to her family and, you know, she was absolutely the reason why. There were plenty of reasons why I found her a good person, but her values were one of the most Important. Every time she used to speak she used to say 'inshallah' - 'God willing' - and I thought, 'here is a woman who has come from a liberal family, who is modern in her outlook, yet these values are instilled inside and help her to be grounded.' Somebody who says 'inshallah' can't be a bad person overall. She is educated, goodlooking and I wanted to be with somebody who had religion as the central point and was independent-minded. It all fitted nicely together.

25 years of marriage later, and we have two lovely children. My daughter has graduated now and started a career with an investment bank. My son is going to graduate next year and hopefully will do something in the field of economics. Both kids are independent, but they also have values instilled inside them, about religion and about the importance of family. These run like threads from my parents to us, to our children - the importance of relationships and the wider family.

Having been settled in Britain for a long time, I didn't want to get married in Bangladesh. I wanted to marry someone where I lived. At that time, a lot of my friends were going abroad to get married, but I felt the need, because we settled here in the UK and we were going to live here until our last day. I wanted to make sure that I married somebody British, who was educated in Britain and who would be able to be a good partner for me in everything that we did. I was quite grateful to have found the person that I wanted to spend the rest of my life with. Even though, when I got married, a lot of people thought I was marrying into a very liberal family - people that I might not be able to cope with, or she might not be able to cope with living in a very conservative family, a family that's come from a village. We have managed to navigate our way through using principles and values. Principles of religion, principles of relationships, roles and responsibilities and things like that. We've managed to create a healthy relationship, and we're here now 25 years on! To say it was tough in the beginning would be an understatement because of the difference in the liberal and conservative culture within the two families. But as I said in the previous chapter, when you get to the village you have to take on certain mannerisms, the way you have to behave and so on - it's the same thing in a relationship as well.

I mentioned about spending Ramadan with my mother and our family together but you might ask, "What of your wife's family? Don't you see them at Ramadan?" Well, we can't really. My father-in-law passed away a few years ago. But after I married my wife and my brother-in-law married too, in the 90s, my mother-in-law and father-in-law emigrated back to Bangladesh. They settled in Dhaka and would come and go every summer, so we never had an opportunity to spend time with them.

My father-in-law was a businessman and, unfortunately, with the Eighties economic crash and ensuing recession, they lost their businesses. After that, he decided that he couldn't rebuild again here in the UK, and chose to go back and just settle in Dhaka. They were happily settled there for many years.

Children and Marriage

My wife is second generation - born and bred in the UK - and considers herself British, so there is the irony that, while I am considered a 'bideshi' in my home village, there's an element of being the 'foreigner from Bangladesh' in my marriage! She often says to me that I follow more Bangladeshi culture than she did, even though, when she was a child, she was taught how to play the harmonium and how to sing the songs of Rabindranath Tagore. But over the years that changed, she stopped playing the harmonium, singing Tagore and became more interested in Islam, Muslim culture, as it enhanced who she is, as a British Bangladeshi female. This aspect of culture took over. That doesn't mean that she has no interest at all but she doesn't play harmonium any longer, but she sometimes hums a Tagore just to be funny.

My daughter is very interested in culture. She loves Pohela Baisakhi type events and she always looks out for things like that. She sees her cousins from her mum's side in Dhaka, who dress up and celebrate various things and she wants to do that, but we haven't got anything that happens here like that. Sometimes her way of showing this interest is when she asks me if there is anything going on that she can go to, or send a message to people saying happy new year, Pohela Baisakh, things like that.

The cultures of my children are very integrated now. British, Muslim, Bengali – all three in one - and I suppose, just like myself, they switch in and out of the ones that they need, at any time. I am guessing that's the same case for most children growing up in the UK today, caught between several different things. If they can balance it right, they will be far richer as individuals and as people. If they lose one, then they have a real loss.

It's like learning languages. If you learn ten languages, you're far richer linguistically. If you have worked in different cultures then you are far richer, (as an employee, as an entrepreneur,) than just being stuck in your own space and then when you lose your job you don't know what you're doing, you don't know what to do, you've been institutionalised or you are just used to one setting, dealing with one type of people. This is why diversity matters.

The question of when our children marry is a common one in Asian households. Do you leave your children to choose for themselves, or do you make arrangements for them? I think the process I went through will be the same process both of my children will likely follow. I think my children's Nani, my wife's mother, will always on the lookout for them, always finding people, but we have not gone down that route of any discussions. I guess the same thing will happen for both of them, which is either the nani or the dadi will keep looking for people and present them to them. Then, if they're up for it, it may happen like that, or, along their own journey they'll pop up with a suggestion and then we will have to consider how to navigate that.

At the end of the day, you want the best person, the best family for your kids, and a relationship that will work. If there is a whole combination of things that are in the right place, then that's good. Otherwise, if it's just built on looks or want to marry a 'highflying professional', then that is going to fizzle out at some point. There has to be a combination of things that both parties believe in and they have to set aside values first, because if they don't then the relationship is unlikely to work. The most important thing is to ensure that Islam is at the heart of a life partner. I am more on the ground of: yes, even if the nanis and the dadis find people, and even if they present suggestions, we need to work through these values, keep these people honest. And these people have to do the same with us.

There are always important questions to ask. Are they criminallyminded? Are they more interested in money? Are they more interested in relationships or status? You've got to work through all of these things. Now, if somebody is found, it may be that they are not always necessarily a 'round wheel', as it were. There may be bits that are not quite round. Similarly, on our side as well – they may find us not entirely round; we may be quite 'square' in parts! We just need to make sure that our parts in the wheel fit enough to make it a wheel, that the chances of breakup are minimised. Because, as we have learnt through the lockdowns, domestic abuse cases have risen. Many couples have realised that they don't fit because they based the relationship on something else, and suddenly being stuck in a house with their partner has caused problems because their values weren't right at the beginning.

Return to Bangladesh?

One of my dreams is that, once the children are settled, we would like to follow in my wife's parents footsteps and move back to Bangladesh. In order for us to do that I would need to shift my work over to a system I could actually run in another country for the winter months. Being there in the winter where it is warmer than in the UK, or to go and spend the winter months in Spain or something like that. It certainly appeals to me for my remaining time on Earth! Winter months in warmer climates, that would be excellent.

Would I bother with Bangladesh at all? I think the answer is yes: the calling is there. It does all depends on health and wellbeing. With my wife having Multiple Sclerosis, these are considerations we have to work out. If I can keep my health straight then we can quite comfortably have a go at the calling to spend more time in Bangladesh. If not every year, then at least some of the time, but this does mean shifting my business over to a more digitally structured system, so that wherever I am I can ensure that there is a at least a small amount of funds coming in to sustain us. Like my father, I am not really inclined to have a wealth creation programme and just hoard the money. What's the point? When you are retired you don't know what you're going to do with it!

For this reason, among others, I am beginning to develop my work as a life coach. I am taking this seriously to properly train myself so that, once my training is complete, I can try to help many more people. Life coaching is a rewarding career to develop and it is a new exciting step in my work. Indeed, it is the culmination of all that I have been through my whole life, inspired, as I have been, by my father and his altruistic principles.

Chapter Eight:
Public Sector to Entrepreneur

Early Days of Work

It has been quite a journey from those early days of beginning work after education to the present time, progressing as an entrepreneur. In this chapter I'd like to explore this story again, thinking about the work life and getting the right balance.

In 1991, I had to leave University because my father was quite ill and we were living in a very small property, in a very over-crowded situation. I had to leave halfway through my first year to get a job, as a clerical officer in the council . This was the era of poll tax and I was in a big treasury department dealing with these issues, clerical activities and sometimes seeing the public at the booths in the town hall. This sometimes meant getting abuse from people. Many of the people waiting to be seen were Asian and when they saw my face they would all queue up in front of my booth. My line manager didn't like that and wanted me to tell the people to queue up along all the booths, but he didn't understand that they wanted to be seen by someone who looks like them and understands their language. If they got seen by one of the other colleagues, they needed to get an interpreter.

I worked there for a while and, to be honest, I didn't feel comfortable. I wasn't really sure if that was the kind of work I wanted to do, shuffling paper and doing admin all day long. In addition to that, I didn't feel comfortable for another reason. My line manager was quite a difficult person, who left me feeling really uneasy every time I used to go into work. In their eyes, I couldn't do anything right. I wasn't sure at the time whether it was that the line manager was being strict and wanted everything to be done in a certain way, or if it was because I was a male and brown. I didn't know if there was an element of prejudice involved in the way I was looked at, or the certain things that were asked of me. I felt more and more uneasy as the days went by and, within nine months, I decided I didn't want to stick around. At that point, as I mentioned earlier, my grandmother, my nani, was taken ill in Bangladesh. I decided to pack in my job and take my mum abroad to see my nani, who was very ill and unlikely to live for long.

Before heading out to Bangladesh, however, I had a job interview for a senior research and development officer position with a housing association. It was called the Oldham Muslim Housing Association and while I was away, I heard that I had been offered the job. My father said that I needed to get back quick in order to take it on.

My grandma died while I was there with her in Bangladesh. She died of bronchitis, caused by years of cooking at the cooking stove, the smoke getting into her lungs every time she would light the fire on the wood under the pots and blow on the fire to make it stronger. All that blowing into the fire meant the smoke damaged her lungs. It was one of the most tragic and saddest moments for me. She lived on her own as a widow, having married off her daughters and having no sons to look after her. It was very sad. As the eldest grandchild, I was given the responsibility to decide where to bury her, so I decided to bury her in a corner by the pond, near the road so that, when people went past, they would pray for her.

New Challenges

I started the new job with the Oldham Muslim Housing Association and I was one of the first employed for the organisation. Another senior research and development officer came on board, plus an admin person and some volunteers. My job was to do research into the housing needs of the Muslim population in Oldham. In addition to that, I also worked with the partner agency, North British Housing Association, who were developing a number of sites for the association. I had to do site visits and support with picking bricks, interiors and things like that. All of a sudden, I was kind of catapulted from being a senior research and development officer to being a development kind of construction officer. Then I had to devise lettings policies and various other policies to get the houses let. So, in that short space of time I did quite a varied amount of different roles, ensuring the organisation was ticking over in the right way. Unfortunately, we didn't have enough money to employ people for those specific different type of tasks and so the pressure fell on me. By 1993 I was suffering burnout.

Because of my burnout I decided to leave that job and go to work for the youth and community section of the education department of Tameside council. They had a project they managed for their local Bangladeshi community, primarily in Hyde, called the Shapla project. I was a community development officer working with the community to provide activities that would empower people and would enable them to access services and jobs that would enhance and develop the community's journey forward. I worked with a lot of young people, with whom I am still in touch with after all these years, who used to play football, so I helped them to run a football competition. I helped one of them go for trials at various football clubs and just generally helped them with job searches and giving them motivation, so they would get out of there and try and create pathway for them to think differently - to their 'inner city' mentality.

In addition to that, I supported a women's group in selling cookery books that they had made prior to my employment. These cookery books would generate money for them to be able to take driving lessons, go on day trips, learn English and things like that. I did that job for eighteen months before my contract ended, and so from there I ended up with the job in Bradford as I explained previously.

I actually didn't want the job. It was a post of being a manager at a community centre - again in the Bangladeshi community, but managed by the council - and that community centre had been very successful in getting a lot of funding, employing lots of people and supporting the Bangladesh community. I went there in the mindset of not wanting the job, and I was actually being really careless with my answers. But the interviewers said I came across as quite headstrong and that's what they wanted for the manager's role - so they gave me the job!

When I got there, I realised that there was a lot that needed sorting out because the place was without a manager for about a year and things were wrong. For example, a great amount of funding returns had not been submitted for accountability, and people were coming and going. There was no proper structure and It was up to me to sort it out. I did what I could, but then I had an operation - a hernia operation – which felt like a cue to me. I tendered my resignation at that point - after five months, - because I didn't really enjoy what I was doing.

Luckily back in Oldham, the area I used to live in, they were designated as a regeneration area and awarded £11.5 million from the Single Regeneration Budget to redevelop the area. Numerous jobs came. There was a community safety officer post, which I successfully applied for. When I took that job opening, my role was to tackle the fear of crime and reduce the incidents of burglary and repeat burglary, giving people confidence by providing personal attack alarms and introducing mortice locks and window locks to properties and businesses. We also did lots of seminars and events to promote how to tackle the fear of crime, and how people should look after their properties so that criminals don't get a chance to get in. All this would reduce petty crime in the area.

It was a very successful project and I was very happily enjoying doing it. But while I was doing that - and as a result of this work, in fact - a vacancy came up. This was an opportunity to move up the ladder a little bit within the team, to become a project officer. The project officer role was to be an assistant to the team leader. This meant that you had a strategic responsibility to assist with creating the delivery plans for the year, to run and manage thematic groups, like the environment theme or the education theme, and each theme would come with a budget of a couple of million pounds. Then, within those themes, you would work with potential delivery partners to develop project proposals. You would then take them to a community panel you had drawn up, and then on to the board. From there, it would go to the development agency for approval.

There was a whole strategic arm to this and, once again, I started to enjoy doing that job and stayed in that role for quite a long time. We did a major amount of regeneration in the area, which in the end won a national award from the British Urban Regeneration Awards. We were not just working as employees but had built a real team spirit. That meant we worked selflessly - even out of our own time - to make sure that more people were engaged, more people benefited from the regeneration, and more people inputted into some of the issues that needed to be solved in the area. A lot of environment improvements took place, jobs were created, external investment came into the area, culture and arts-related activities took place. I was in charge of small grants and every year we supported at least 60 applications, up to the maximum of £2000, to do little projects in the area that would make an impact. Some of these projects would then become larger projects. It was almost like a seed-funding scheme and I was very keen to ensure that as many people as possible accessed the scheme, received funding and did what they needed to do. Even if they failed, at least it's an opportunity to see something. As long as there was accountability, there wasn't really a problem.

That was really good because I remember some groups used to say to me, "Oh we never knew that we would be eligible to get this money. And even if we were, we probably thought you guys were bureaucrats so you would make it difficult for us to access this money. But you've gone out of your way to make sure that you guided us, given us the right guidelines, given us the right thinking to make sure that our applications were right for them to be assessed by the panels". I guess the whole motto of how I worked there was that the funds came for the benefit of the people in the area, whether it would be physical regeneration or social regeneration. So, we were there as caretakers of that fund and we should be managing it in such a way that every penny was used properly and the people were the ones to benefit at the end of the day. This was my whole notion and we were very successful in that team, leading up to winning the award.

I carried on working in regeneration and moved into another programme - SRB63 - which was in an area called Glodwick. No sooner had I moved into this area, within a year, there was the race riots of 2001. And so obviously, even though that area had only half of what Westwood had, which was £6 million, that area needed much more money. But by that time the government had slashed the regeneration budget and gave to more areas around the country. That was why I then I moved into another programme called SRB6 which was a much bigger area, with a budget of £21 million. Similarly, we did a lot of work around social, cultural, economic, education and environmental regeneration in the area, with our whole motto to benefit people.

I remember going to a community panel meeting in Hollinwood. I'd been used to working in the Asian community, but this was not an Asian community, it was a white English neighbourhood. I remember the first meeting I went to. Quite a few people looked at me and you could tell they thought, 'He can't be the officer, he's brown!' There were a few people there who didn't even make eye contact with me and they kept saying, "No, no, we can't make any decisions until Shirley comes in the next meeting." And I was like, "No, no, I am the designated officer!'

They weren't having any it, some of them, not all. It was interesting for me to observe because, eventually, they realised that I was human and those who knew me were okay with me. It was just those who hadn't had any interaction with somebody who was brown before, who were having some issues. It transpired that, later on, after they interacted with me for a number of years, they realised how I go out of my way and I am not just a worker with a job description, but that I do actually go beyond to support and assist them, to make them understand certain things. They actually really enjoyed having me attend meetings and having me provide that support. At the point when I was leaving SRB6 they were the people who were pleading with me not to leave, and saying how I needed to stay and carry on!

Change in Direction

At that point though, I thought I've done regeneration for nearly nine years and I needed to move on. To be honest, regeneration-funded programmes are exciting at the beginning because you're creative, you're creating new ideas, looking at new things, putting things together, putting projects together and big money and big events. It's all very exciting, monitoring and verification and all that. You're going in, checking in, auditing, monitoring, verification visits regularly. It was really quite exciting and, in terms of skill development, it was very good because you're doing a whole range of vertical skills that you would not have done if, say, you were in just one job. If you are a town planner, for example, you would just be looking at planning applications or something. This was like the whole range of tasks you had to do and you learnt so much in terms of communication. Towards the end of these schemes - the 'closure period' - things can be really boring and tedious. I start to lose my motivation.

I applied for a number of jobs within the council and never got a look-in, so I became rather frustrated. I couldn't figure out why I wasn't getting a chance, given that my skills had developed to a very high level - already being involved in three major regeneration programmes and having the ability to do everything needed, communicate and deliver at every level. I couldn't figure out why I wasn't getting interviews for other jobs and It was easy to become despondent. I lost interest, I lost motivation and I thought maybe somebody's putting a block on my name; they didn't want me going for these jobs, didn't want me to go any further. In the end I just walked out.

I left my SRB6 Job, and I didn't have a job to go to. My wife was getting really stressed, "How are we going to live? What are we going to live on?" I kept saying, "Don't worry something will come up,"

I had the belief that when you do good and you are constantly giving –having been involved with all these voluntary and charity activities - that something will come up. It just so happened a friend of mine was in the property business and I was talking to his son about marketing. They had this really pleasant restaurant. I was telling him about marketing, just theorising marketing ideas with creative thoughts, and the son - who must have been quite excited by what I said - went and mentioned it to his father. His father said to me, "Why don't you come and market my restaurant? How much do you charge?" I had to think on my feet really quickly and tell him a figure - which I did and he agreed!

I started doing some marketing for this restaurant and I thought, 'Okay this is fine, this is bringing in about a quarter of what I would have earned normally, but at least it's some pounds.' After about four weeks, my friend's father said to me, "Why don't you come and market my property business?" I was absolutely being honest when I answered and said, "Look, I don't really know much about marketing. I do like to theorise a lot but practically I have not done much marketing. Not marketing in its true sense." But his response was, "No, no, you have done very well with the restaurant. Do something similar and improvise, put the word out and get more people to be interested in what we are doing".

I joined him on a salary and, again, it was less than I was used to - around half of what I probably would have got with the job I left with the council. In the end I just took it. I had these two roles now: one to market the restaurant, one to market the property business. Soon I realised he wanted a marketeer, but he also wanted a business development person, so I tried to combine the two roles into one. Having left the council, where I had structured systems and processes and working to a routine, now here was something where every day I had to think about new strategies, new markets, new ways to open up business for the restaurant and property business. It exciting because we were looking at Ireland, Cardiff, Bradford, down south, and we were engaging people in all those different areas. All of a sudden, from having lost my motivation, I was really excited again. We were working hard, and the business was growing. The job was in financial services and grew so fast that the company went from three or four staff to about twenty staff within the space of a year. I was enjoying myself because I was crafting some of those journeys and my friend, the CEO, was implementing those and taking some major risks which were playing out well.

Then came the recession and it washed the company away. Suddenly I had no job and again, my wife said, "What are we going to do? You need to get a proper job". And I said, "Yeah, of course, something will come along!" Thankfully, a month later, I went for a job interview in Leeds, to work for Involve, Yorkshire and Humber - It was previously called the Yorkshire and Humber Regional Forum. It was a third sector umbrella body which used to support third sector organisations across Yorkshire and Humber, and it was community, voluntary, charity, and not-for-profit. I got a job as a programme director which was rather nice because I never had a director title in my name - I felt, 'Oh this is good - good pay'!

The only problem was having to travel there every morning. It was an remarkable amount of pain. After about eight months I decided to travel by driving to Marsden, leave the car there, get on a train to Huddersfield and then go to Leeds. Then there was a further twenty-minute walk to the office but that, at least, was better than driving two hours there and two hours back, as I had been doing, because it gave me the opportunity to read many books which I thoroughly enjoyed. That's when I got back into reading again. The more I read, the more my interest in reading grew, the more my brain and my imagination began to grow and I could apply the learning from reading in my job and in my personal development.

That time in Leeds was a nice break for me. I had gone back into a job, after spending a year being creative and thinking differently, and I was in charge of one other member of staff. Then another member came on board. My job was to provide programmes that would strengthen the voluntary sector, particularly the black minority ethnic sector, and to create programmes that would develop them further. A lot of governance-related matters, communication, goal setting, visioning, that sort of thing. We launched a newspaper for the sector called BME Voice, which was very professionally done and delivered to all the stakeholders around Yorkshire and the Humber. We raised the profile of the BME third sector using the newspaper, and all the good news stories that used to go into it, but we also did a lot of training to get them to think differently. That was also a contracted job. It finished in 2011 and so I came back to Oldham -yet again! - without a job. Once again, I had no work but, because I had this belief inside me that I'll get something somewhere again, I went for a number of interviews. Which I never got! I thought maybe getting a job through an interview was not the right thing for me. One of them I went to twice and failed to secure the job, for the position of private sector fundraising officer for Madhlo - an Oldham youth zone project. But the chief executive and the chair called me in and said, "You did a great interview. Some of the ideas you came up with, can you come and develop them?" I went working for them two days a week to develop these ideas, and we did in fact develop plenty. During this time we did a 5km run (getting 70 people involved), and hosted a big dinner for the Asian business leaders and many other initiatives.

Again, that was only a six-month contract, so after that I got another job with the Oldham racial equality partnership. It was a community development project and it was almost like going back twenty years with that job. Things that I had done two decades before were particularly true of that job.

After that I decided that I didn't want to work anymore for anyone else. I wanted to become an entrepreneur and whilst I was doing all these other jobs, I started listening to a lot of motivational CDs, watching inspirational people on YouTube, looking at how they prepare themselves and how they set their goals and how they do things differently. I was repeating mantras to myself and I would also repeat them to people around me just to see how they react. I thought to myself, 'You know I've got to make something of myself', but then I lost confidence again. I ended up with another job in the private sector, in a medical services company. When I was interviewed over dinner by the chief executive, I was genuinely overwhelmed by his kindness and desire to grow his business. But for me, more importantly, it was his mannerisms and kindness that attracted me to want to work for this company as head of marketing. My job was to really take their company to another level in terms of promoting it to general practices and doctors to attract their interest in the company, because it was a service provider and it needed referrals from doctors.Once again, I just thought, 'You know what? I really need to do something for myself.' I didn't like the 9-to-5 anymore because things had changed in my head, during my time working for this medical company. Luckily, I built a good relationship with the founder and CEO who was like a big brother, and soon his words of wisdom had helped me to gain my confidence back again, even though I no longer worked for the company. I was motivated to go forward by this inspiration-al person to become the person I needed to become. I must show gratitude to Dr Tariq Chauhan for his wisdom and motivation, which he continues to give me to the present day.

I came out of there and set up my first marketing company. I had be-come a fullyfledged entrepreneur now, so I had to do everything on my own. I had to set the goal, I had to set the vision, had to set the objectives and actions and I had to go look for work and pitch to business owners, to present myself in a certain way. Luckily, I started attracting small busi-nesses that wanted to do well, retail businesses, medical businesses and hospitality businesses. Soon I started attracting quite a number of them. I had a different rate card for each one of them because that depended on what they wanted. Some wanted just social media marketing, some wanted integrated communication, some wanted to enter into the Asian market because they didn't have enough of that segment, some just wanted gener-al communication, and so on.

I've realised that I have the capability and that I should never under-estimate myself about becoming a self-made entrepreneur. I have been working on that path now, doing consultancy, for a number of years. I am also a regional consultant for Strengthening Faith Institution programmes based in London which works with faith-based organisations to help them to become stronger, through stronger governance, through stronger risk management, through safeguarding, through health and safety, teach-er-training and, at present, delivering Covid compliance, Covid19 compli-ance officers, webinars, and doing risk assessments for places of worship. As a result of all of this, I find myself as an entrepreneur now. I'm not a public servant anymore, but whilst I've changed my line of work, I have maintained and continued to do my giving and charitable work. Hence, the main idea of this book – 'The gift of giving' – with more and more businesses interested in working with me now. Some businesses want to work with me because they want someone to connect them, some business-es want marketing, and some just want to talk to me for advice. From all of this, I am sort of transforming my consultancy into more of a coaching business so that I can reach more people. I can give to more people, listen to what they need, what they want, and I can help them to facilitate them-selves to where they want to be. I can help them find where the blockages are and unblock them.

Going into the future, this whole notion of entrepreneurship, it's really become quite real and it's amazing how people trust you, how people re-spect you and believe in you. They know the fact that you have the capa-bility to help them, support them, assist them, guide them and make them better, make their business better. Ultimately, they trust you to guide them in the right direction. Without trust, there is no business. Therefore my journey as an entrepreneur is built on values as those credentials have been the pillars on which my business is built.

Naturally, I like to work with small businesses because it gives me great satisfaction in knowing that a small amount of change or transformation makes a big difference to them. When I see that change, I know they talk highly of me to some of their other friends who are in business. Then through word of mouth endorsement, an acknowledgement for what I do, more people want to work with me. But I realise that individually, I can't take it any further, unless I start to employ people. I haven't crossed that bridge yet – although I am at the entrance - other than the fact that I did employ a couple of people for a short period, but unfortunately one of them had cancer, and had to leave, the other one also had some illness, so had to leave too.

Now I am ready to transform myself as an entrepreneur, to become a life and business coach. Having trained and completed all the preparatory work, I'm looking forward to a future of helping people in this way and have already begun the work. At the present time I am in my trial period and already have several clients. Some are individuals who have life goals that they want to achieve, while others are small, independent businesses. The work has been amazing! Since beginning my trial work, all of my clients have already seen results, thanks to the early coaching. The future is glowing!

What I charge for my services varies from client to client. For small businesses I typically have a flat fee, but for businesses on different levels, depending on what they want, I have a sliding scale. I won't work with any company or individual if I don't feel comfortable with their aims. I have to check their belief systems and values because if those are not in the correct order, no matter what kind of conversation I have with them and no matter what they tell me, they will turn around and do something different. That might then give me a bad reputation for not being a good coach, which is obviously not something I want to see.

My goal in relation to coaching is to be able to facilitate that change and transformation in a whole range of people, rather than just doing consultancy for a couple of clients here and there. I'd rather reach more people around the world, to be truly global in what I do. I think now I have come this far, I need to reach out and give a wide range of people what I have learnt . The gift of giving should not be limited but shared widely, whatever the gift is.

Thoughts on Being a Life Coach

The problem with coaching is that often it can be full of glamour and glitz, when you see the coaches online - all kind of American-style nonsense really, to be honest. You can present a kind of rubbish that people come away with a big buzz but several months later it all comes to nothing because there's no substance. I initially got interested and hooked by that American razzmatazz and the buzz that these guys create and the way they create it. I studied it very carefully and saw they create a funnel; and that funnel is created so that once you're in, once your head is in there, your body is going to go there too. Once you have done the taster day or discovery day, you will buy into another course and at the end of that you'll then buy another course. You know by the end of the day if you benefit from it, that's great, but if you're the type of person that just gives them the money and not feel the benefit from it afterwards, then that will be a waste of time for you. Perhaps some people do benefit from the razzmatazzy type of thing, it's there certainly for a reason – to hook you in.

If you said to me, come have fish and chips or come and have vegetables, I'll go for the fish and chips because I won't go for the goodness, I'll go for the stuff that's not good for me but that is tasty. Similarly, that kind of razzmatazz, it's not good for everybody, but some people who go to these things gain some benefit. I have studied all of those things and numerous videos on YouTube on how it is a classical technique to lure people in, to part with money.

The thing is - from my point of view, where I am now - to become a life coach or a guide for people, to find their way, it is not essential that you do that kind of course. You could do things more systematic like neurolinguistic programming or you could go on a communications course and learn about the art of communicating and marry those two things with your life experience. Then just understand the difference between mentoring and coaching. As a strong believer of my religion, I believe that Allah has given every person their rizq and that they need to find their rizq by doing whatever is necessary, as long as it is not illegal or immoral. My role in helping people is something I believe has been pre-destined. I am just navigating towards it, with help of the creator.

Once you got those things in place, then you've got the ingredients of what you are, who you are, and what your ability to deliver a coaching session is. Then obviously you are structuring your session in a way, that it is organised, it is recorded, it is accountable and then you follow it through. Most of the work has to be done by the individual who needs to make the changes or who needs to set a goal, reach that goal, do the things that will get them there, and avoid what won't. It's hard, it's really hard, for some people, because many are set in their ways and some of the barriers that they may need to avoid they can't get away from .

To make a transformation they've got to make these hard decisions and you have to help them to see the opportunity in what they are trying to do. As a coach you are almost like a mother figure, or a father figure You are navigating your child to a better life and you just have to understand and read the person, where they are what they are saying, what they want and be able to facilitate the conversations in a very realistic manner, in a timely manner, as well as for them to be able to see those little changes. I think that in the end the people who are looking for genuinely real good coaches are looking for people who will not be the razzmatazz type, but somebody who they can sit with and they can use to cry on their shoulder. There is a difference between counselling, coaching and mentoring - some people can get confused about which one is which, but as long as you know the core principles that differ and then you are getting them to make those changes and using the right kind of positive language and positive attributes in order to help them to move on - that's the way you see the success.

This has been my approach with clients and, I have to say, I've yet to see any sign of failings. Three of my independent business clients have seen a massive shift in success in their businesses already, and at least one other will see success very soon. Two of the individuals who have lifelong goals are well on the way to setting them up the right way, and I am guiding them carefully through my conversations. I truly believe I am doing all the right things to help others achieve their goals, ambitions and successes; and I'm certainly looking forward to helping even more.

Chapter Nine: Opportunities

Opportunity and Rizq

Throughout my life I've had this great belief that there are opportunities for every individual. As a Muslim I believe that every individual is born with their opportunity. In Arabic it's called rizq, and I've mentioned it a few times in previous chapters. If people faithfully believe that notion then there are plenty of opportunities out there for people to take advantage of, to make use of, to go and find.

This doesn't mean you have to be a Muslim for this law to be true. I think what you will find is that in every faith, there is something similar; that your provisions are provided. I don't know about if somebody has no belief; but then maybe their non-belief has some belief in how they acquire things and how they see this journey of life for themselves. But there will be some sort of belief in there. In the non-belief in God or non-belief in religion, they will have their own sense of belief as well about what they believe they can achieve. It might just be from themselves. It applies across the board - this whole notion of provision and rizq - regardless of faith, and I think most people who understand comparative faith will know that these concepts are very similar in all the different books that have come down the ages.

But what happens when you have a belief based on faith, then it's almost like it gives you the confidence to know what you have. When you have faith, you believe that provisions are there because you come from somewhere, you are somebody, you're going somewhere. That therefore makes it easier and gives you the confidence to know that you can actually go out there and live off the land, or find the opportunity in a factory, or find the opportunity in the corporate world or even if you turn into a monk or something you've still got your opportunities available within those surroundings. That's where I think, as somebody who has belief, I believe that my provisions are there, and they'll come in the right way and right time. I just need to facilitate myself and navigate myself in the right way to be able to attract what's been granted for me.

Often, I find people expect something to land in their lap and perhaps wouldn't go and try to find it for themselves. Whether it's going through an academic process, or preparing themselves for something later on, or going through an entrepreneurship process whereby they learn something that can be turned into a bigger opportunity, or just having a creative brain which allows them to see opportunity from adversity.

There are many quotations I have read over the years to help me to understand the whole notion of opportunities that exist out there in the wide world. One of my favourite ones is Albert Einstein who says, "In the middle of difficulty, lies opportunity". We are in the midst of a very difficult time at the time of writing - the Coronavirus pandemic - and I know there are people, a lot of people, losing their jobs. There will be a lot of people who will be affected mentally by this situation. However, there are other people I know of who have seized the opportunity, or seized the moment, to craft out new opportunities and be able to develop new ideas, new businesses, new products, new services and new ways of doing things. They will be the ones, once the pandemic is put aside or is over, who will benefit and reap the rewards of having a creative brain and being able to look at this doom and gloom situation while, at the same time, look at what can they offer to the world as a product or a service that will benefit people.

At the end of the day, the offering is what benefits people out there and, in the entrepreneurial context, it could be a product, or it could be a service as well. So, I often say to people that, when people come and talk to me about either not having a job or their business is not going well or the health is not good or something is not right around them, I say to them that there is always something better when you open a different door, but you've got to know that a different door actually does exist.

Often what people ask me is, what if you do not have enough money, or not having enough opportunities to create money for yourself and family? Then I always tell them a favourite saying of mine: if you look closely, there could be opportunity hidden in your garden. You don't even know, you don't look for it, you can't even dig for it. It's the metaphor for going out, looking at things differently, looking at things that can become opportunities, that can be turned into opportunities.

People will often shy away from exploring further opportunities because they see it is as quite hard work. Hard work then can be a wall towards achieving somebody's goal, achieving someone's desired goal, because hard work comes in the way. And because of hard work coming in the way, it holds them back from something. Maybe they're probably two steps away from achieving something, after putting in a certain amount of effort? Unfortunately, they just don't see it that they were probably two steps away from reaching that opportunity – the very thing they wanted to have for a long time.

So, I always say to people that if you truly and sincerely and honestly want something - and you've got clarity in your thoughts, you've got clear vision of what it is that you want to establish, how you want to establish, and how you want to seek the opportunity - you will find a way to get there. Often what happens is I find that people don't have the clear vision of where they see themselves, so they see themselves as really fit and healthy or they don't see themselves as really doing very well financially, or they don't see themselves being charitable and philanthropic in a certain way. Then they are not going to reach that space.

I think it is absolutely vital they have a clear vision of where they are going and then plan the route map to get to that vision turned into a reality. A lot of people just float around. I know a lot of people who will be academically really good, then they'll get a job after a few years and realise it's not for them. They are seeking for something else they need to do, seeking for something more fulfilling, which is not being given to them by a corporate job. When I chat to them, they say things like, "Well I have done the education, I wanted to be a certain corporate type of person and I realise I am not fulfilled. I want to go out and do some philanthropic work. I want to go and help people. I know that's the greatest amount of satisfaction I will get if I do that because once I did something similar in my corporate job and I felt really good". So, people are always looking.

They are always looking for new opportunities for self-fulfilment as well as new opportunities for entrepreneurship or even just being - just for personal satisfaction. What I am saying is that there is enough opportunity out there in the world. People really need to have a look at it in a certain way, have the passion, the drive and the commitment to be able to do something. I know of people who have created huge amount of opportunity out of a very simple idea and these simple ideas are easy for you to miss because you are blinded by something or you have tinted glasses; you look at opportunity as a big thing and you miss where the little things can become a big opportunity - a little service to society, or a little bit of a product, can be something that you can develop so it becomes something phenomenal and a brand for whatever you are trying to do.

People always make excuses and it's never their fault. It was someone else's fault that they are not getting the opportunity to achieve something. I always say to people that they really need to look at their own journey, look at how they can start to address some of their needs and not blame others. But the blame culture exists today. Getting people out of that way of thinking is key to any success.

I've tried to open many a door for people, but the question really isn't about opening doors: it's about whether that person is keen to go through that door once opened and find what they are looking for. At the end of the day, it's only them that can get to where they want to get to, but they need to walk through the door. Or go through the window – whichever metaphor you prefer! Some people I've known through my many years of interaction rely too much on someone else to give them their opportunity on a plate, and they will go round being a follower hoping to get some scraps.

People also don't want to put time in. Time is a really crucial aspect of looking at opportunities. People feel that it will just happen, and then they don't want to put in the time in. All this perception of time - time management issues are very important! I feel that when I talk to people they would rather just look around. Sometimes you'll get people who will think about things and believe that by thinking about things that they've achieved something, or they are getting nearer to the goal, because they are just constantly thinking about it, or planning, or writing down things instead of taking action. So, people who actually identify something - and then they take action - are the ones who usually find the opportunities they are looking for. It is people that don't take action that are the ones who don't find the opportunity.

The reason I am reflecting on all of this is because, in my lifetime, I recognise that there is ample opportunity out there for me. It's up to me to identify what opportunity I need to seize, how I need to go and grab it and make it happen; taking that leap of faith, taking that action, and make it work. And it's happened! It has worked for me. In terms of my work life, I've never been out of work for long – I've either worked for someone or I've worked for myself. Working for myself is all about creating the opportunity, because getting a job for me was relatively easy - you fill in a number of applications, you get a number of interviews, you end up with a job that pays you and that's it - whereas being an entrepreneur, I am having to create my own opportunities and I am having to look at areas that I can contribute to, that will benefit either an individual or a business. Whether it be through business marketing, or through guidance, whether it's through connecting business people, connecting individuals, or other individuals, so they can make things happen.

Recently I have been connecting a PR person with a number of individuals who need to be publicized and I've connected at least three people during the lockdown with my PR person, who is helping them to reach mainstream media and developing their own message for their own causes. Similarly, I see that I can develop opportunities out of nothing because when I see a need for something to happen, l develop the idea and I'll bring around people who can contribute - it is beneficial for everybody.

If I can find opportunities out of nothing, if I can develop ideas out of nothing that then became my opportunities, then I believe that every single person out there who is looking for the ideal opportunity can find what they are looking for. It's just that they are probably not looking in the right place. It's just that they are probably not thinking about it in the right way. It's just that they're probably measuring their desire against other people and that's certainly not the right way to do it. They've got to look internally at their own ability, their own skills base and their own interest, and then work using that rather than comparing themselves to others out there. The more people compare, the more they get lost. The more they get lost, the more they lose their authenticity - who they are and their uniqueness. Then their idea doesn't develop, or they never reach their goal. They never see the opportunity that exists because of who they are. The law of attraction doesn't work with them because they are always looking at someone else, they're always comparing themselves to someone else.

I am a true believer in my rizq then, and I truly believe that there is something out there for me – at least one, if not more than one opportunity out there for me - which is why I say the theme of this chapter is 'opportunities, opportunities, opportunities galore'! There is ample opportunity out there; you have to, honestly and sincerely, put your hand on your heart and decide what it is that you're about, what is your purpose?; and if you are doing philanthropic stuff, what is your purpose? Find that purpose, then go after it and the opportunities will open up to you, the doors will appear - though you've got to know which doors to open or keep shut. Similarly, if you are an entrepreneur, if you're in business, you're creating an idea, you're creating a product and you're looking for the next thing that might be useful for you, helpful to you and gives you that freedom of space and time and money, then you've got to really look deep inside you and think, 'What am I good at doing? What am I creating for the benefit of the people?' Because, at the end of the day, whether you're a philanthropist, or an entrepreneur or just an individual - everything that you do - you have to look at how does that benefit people? If it benefits people you've got something special that you can create and that's your opportunity.

Sometimes people will say, "Well you know, I don't have the skills, I don't have the contacts, I don't have the money". They will always find excuses to not get up and do, to create the opportunity or find the opportunity. Another quote I like is Richard Branson who used to say, "If somebody offers you an amazing opportunity but you are not sure you can do it, say yes – then learn how to do it later!". I think often people who learn - often through trial and error - are the more successful people because they believed in something and committed to something. They realised they didn't know how they were going to achieve it, but they found a way; and that is when you are at your best, when you are thinking because then you are really, really up against the wall or something, and you got to climb that wall like Spiderman - you've got to find a way to get through that wall, get around it, or get over it. That's when people are at their best - when they are thinking about crafting out an opportunity.

There are opportunities hidden everywhere - even failure is an opportunity! People need to recognise that. Often people imagine that if they've failed, they're at the gloomiest end of the world. Actually, in America, the whole notion of failing six times before you're successful is kind of a well-researched thought process. I think in Britain, we're a bit more tight-lipped about it, a bit more reserved. I know hundreds of people, at least, who have failed a number of times, bounced back and created opportunities out of thin air. I know people who have literally just set up businesses, done really well, and then suddenly lost everything; six months later they create something out of nothing, with something they know nothing about. But what they do know is how to attract the right people to help them to achieve what they want. They may not necessarily know every little detail about everything - whether it's technology, whether it's marketing or whether it's financial planning; they may not know any of that stuff - but what they have is the knack of making use of the brains out there in order to create their opportunity. They've created a massive amount of businesses, or even giving causes, out of thin air. Anyone who has a creative brain and has the courage to step forward is always likely to succeed.

I know of people, at this moment in time during a pandemic, who are British Bangladeshis but are in Bangladesh right now and haven't been able to come back. Yet they've used their time to plant thousands of trees around their villages; they have used their time to feed thousands of people. What they've done, in each case, is called for help from people they know around the world who have made donations. One guy was able to facilitate feeding, giving food packs to thousands of people, during the initial periods of the pandemic and Ramadan, and then just continued from there. Again, this is just somebody who sat there thinking, 'I've got a lot of time on my hands. I have a lot of people who are going to go hungry. What do I do? I haven't got the kind of money personally to give to them', so they just called out, people joined in and a new initiative was born.

There are people out there, who have the ability in terms of creative ideas, who can create something out of nothing. It's just having that self-belief in the first place. And if people have that self-belief, then they can quite easily achieve their dreams and make them happen. They will make these goals happen and they will see more opportunity than an ordinary person sees because they have a creative brain. It's very important to have such an open mind and creative brain.

Helping Others Help Themselves

Practically, how does this apply in the real world? When I talk to people, I am always very keen to listen to their journey, their background, where they come from, what their interests have been in the past, where they worked, what kind of business they've had, and so on; just getting what kind of family background they are from and what motivates them, what interest them. What often happens is that when you listen to somebody and ask them these questions and listen to the answers, you often find information within that you can then use as bullet points to put back to them to say, "Well clearly you've said something here and this is essentially what you think - that this is something you're heading towards". Then people usually have the answers themselves and they speak these answers in the conversations. It's just making them believe that this is essentially the purpose of where they are heading, and that purpose will then open up the opportunity.

If people are feeling a bit lost, the answers are actually within them. I try to facilitate them to think about their own answers they've given and home in on some of them; to try and facilitate that for them to take it forward to create the next opportunity or create the purpose, so that they've got something genuinely purposeful that they can hang on to. And often that involves talking about their overall vision, overall legacy: Is your legacy a big corporation that you want to leave behind for your children? Is your legacy that you want to be known as a philanthropist? Is your legacy that you want to be known for something in particular? What are you wanting to leave behind? Or do you just want to float around? And more often than not, people will want to say, "We want to do this, because of that." It's helping them to identify why they do what they do, and then helping them to take action afterwards.

That doesn't mean there aren't limitations or boundaries to goals, of course. There are limitations and not everyone's the same. Everyone's different. So, as well as everyone having similar patterns of who they are, each one will have their own underlying limitations and they have to acknowledge that. Having said that, for example, if you were a writer, say, and wanted to buy an island and that was your entire purpose in life, then how would you go and do it? Obviously, you would have to write many more books or have a whole stream of a couple of hundred thousand people coming to you to write their books for them! Then you would have to premium out of them or create some sort of a conglomerate and get shareholding monies until you have enough to buy an island. After all, that's like being Richard Branson or Mark Zuckerberg, and is just what they did themselves. Richard Branson started selling records in market stores and all that led to where he is now. It is possible, but it's not necessarily by just selling those records. I haven't read his biographies, but clearly selling records started him off and he obviously met the right people along the way that believed in what he was doing and would have either given him a few words of wisdom or given him a few pounds to support him along his way.

And that's what people need: they need people with the right kind of words of wisdom to guide them along, to give them the confidence, to know that there is a fall-back position and also help them to see things that they may be clouded by their own negative self or being very unrealistic. Then you need backers, and backers who will back you financially as well, should you need it. Again, knowing that sometimes you don't need it, but knowing that you can have those backers who will back your dreams also helps you to build that confidence to be able to say you can map out an entire process of the next thirty years of where you're heading in terms of your overall goal and begin this with knowing you have enough backing.

I'll give an example of people who are particularly like this. In my travels through Bangladesh I have come across people who are relatively poor, with relatively lower life aspirations and perhaps lower levels of opportunity. I've sat with a few of them and actually explained to them that in order for them to be self-sustainable and successful they should not always be asking for hand-outs. What they should be asking for is support for themselves to do something - whether it's weaving, whether it's crafts, whether it's having a shop, whether it's selling someone else's products - they should create an action-based opportunity and they should ask people they normally ask for hand-outs for donations or loans, so that they can create something that will be long-lasting and sustainable. True to my conversations, some of them, over the years, have done that and they have gone from being in want to another place quite, quite different. They've created a local business and they have grown that business, because initially their thought process was within their own village; now, they are taking their product elsewhere. They know they're expanding their geography and at some point, if they create a bigger processing of what they are doing, they might shift to bigger cities and even out of the country.

That's how somebody needs to think and get their mindset sorted out, in order for them to achieve their goals as opposed to having all these limiting beliefs. There are limitations but the limitations can be overcome by having the right kind of mechanisms in place, the right kind of support mechanism and the right kind of networks in place to be able to bounce off and move on.

Everyone will have a different kind of framework depending on where they are and who they are. If I say, from my point of view, "How do I do it?", I have a belief, so my first thing is that I need to have a belief in something. If I wanted to do a bike ride across Bangladesh then I need to have that belief that it is possible, that it is realistic. Once I have a belief in something then I have to generate the idea, or create the idea, or craft it; almost like drawing it out and looking at it. Then I need to find all the things I need to put in place for it to happen.

For example, say I wanted to publish a book – like this one! I needed to have this belief that it is possible for me; that there is enough material inside of me to be able to create this book. Then think about the idea - how can this be done? And once I've thought about it, then I've got to decide whether I am capable of writing it or if I've got people around me who can help me to write it and then help me to publish it or to promote it, for me to get it out and do on and so forth. Everything has to be very crystal clear in my head about the journey of this particular opportunity – the opportunity of creating my own book that will go out into the world.

If I didn't have all of those things in place - if I just had the belief - I would have simply sat there with the belief in my head; if I didn't have the ideas, if I didn't have the third stage of having all the ingredients in the right place. Whether its money, whether it's myself, or talking to other people in the literary world and talking to all my business friends and talking to the Manchester museum and places like that - the libraries and schools and cultural organisations, both here and across the pond – It all leads me to think, 'Okay well, you step back and think what's the point in writing this journal? Is it just for my kids to read, my family to read? Or is it because there is a great opportunity for my story to be told all over and naturally, in a realistic world? Perhaps it's not something that everybody is going to read, but there is a certain portion of the world that will be interested in knowing what's in it and they benefit from it. This is the purpose of why I'm writing this book.' People have to go through this stage. It is different for each person, but they have to go through it.

The reason why people are not able to find their opportunity is because often they are afraid. They are afraid of making mistakes, they're afraid of losing. I think evil also comes in the way for some people. They don't want to show their weaknesses and they don't want to start something and fail and then start again and fail. All that plays negatively in people's self-talk and people's minds. That's why they've not stepped up to doing something that they are capable of doing.

I personally think whatever I put my mind to I achieve - whether it's charitable stuff, when I've set my mind on something, whether it's enterprising business - when I've set my mind on something I'll go ahead and do it and I'll achieve it with the help of Allah. I need to completely believe in something - the subject - and I need to create that Idea, and then when going to action, find who is out there who can help me to do the stepping-stone activity towards reaching what I want to get to. I totally believe in the fact that the notion of you're always six steps away from the next person you want to talk to and there's always somebody out there who knows somebody who can guide you to, get you to where you need to get to.

And, inshallah, you will.

Muj – 'Bhai'

I know a Bengali man very well,
Where he'll be in ten years' time, who can tell?
He works very hard, he has vision and thought, He has certain quali-
ties which cannot be bought.

I first met him in 1996,
Since then, we've enjoyed many a trick!

He was the man who took me abroad,
To a village in Bangladesh, where his father was born.

Singerkach is the name of this gram, Mujahid Khan is the name of
this man.

I first met him at the S.R.B.,
Little did I know what the future would be.

His father is very well known in this town,
While Muj Bhai has a cap and a gown.

He's been responsible for changing a few lives, He's also helped to
make us wise.

So here's to the future, Muj…Amar Bondu, Let's hope it's good…for
me, and…for you!

Phil Buckley Q.P.M.
2004

Acknowledgements

I am thankful to my late father, my inspiration, my role model who guided us to become better human beings. His wisdom was presented in a way which made sure it was engrained in our hearts and minds. Without him, all of this would not have been possible. My mother, who continues to support me and is always praying for my wellbeing; my mother's blessings are a huge source of protection for me.

I would especially like to thank my brothers, Moshahid and Motahir, for being understanding and supportive throughout my journey. Moshahid and I remember the times when we were young, having lots of pillow fights in our spare time; that was so much fun. Such a gentleman in the family. Motahir was the baby in the family, who has grown into a mature man following in my father's academic footsteps.

I would like to thank my sisters, Shamsun and Tahera, remembering how I cared for them after they were born, seeing them grow into wonderful, sincere and helpful women who are totally devoted to keeping a strong family unit.

I have been blessed with an amazing life partner, my wife Tahmena, who has been everything I wanted in a life partner; someone who is loving, caring, kind and understanding. I have been blessed too with two children, Syra and Mohsin, who have inherited lots of values and traits from my father and mother. They are a blessing and a gift. I want to thank them for their understanding, spending so much time away from home doing community activism, charity work and being on call for people who need support with numerous issues in their daily lives, but importantly, trying my best to continue my father's legacy. They have grown into wonderful, sincere, conscientious young people, and inshallah, achieving their dreams.

All my extended families, both here in Britain and in Bangladesh, have been so loving and caring towards me, that words cannot express my gratitude and affection towards them. It is through their love and affection that I have such wonderful experiences and memories.

I am a socially-driven person, which has allowed me to meet so many people on my journey so far, and who I have met through my childhood, profession, tours, community work, philanthropy, politics and socially.

Ever since my father became ill and asked me to represent him at various functions, I started to enjoy meeting new people and socialising, developing friendships with people from diverse backgrounds, built on respect and common purpose. Some of my friends are no longer the same people and I am happy that they played a role in my journey. But those who have remained the same are a blessing for me.

I would also like to thank the following two people for their unconditional support in my journey: first Kashif Ashraf, my best friend who has been a witness to everything that I have been through; and my dear friend, the late Phil Buckley QPM, whose constant words of encouragement, motivation and support are engrained inside me.

I am grateful to everyone who helped me write this book as it has been done at a fast pace starting at the first lockdown and finished by the third. My special thanks goes to: Ken Powell, Les Howarth, Farhad Ahmed, Dr Musharaf Hussain, Dr Shamim Miah, Saleh Uddin Talukdar, Dr Nazrul Islam, Amin B Choudhury, Miznaur Rahman Mizan, Shafi Ahmed, Fakrul Choudhury, Mashukul Hoque, Obaidul Islam, Humayra Begum, Dewan Rahdi, Dewan Mahdy, Mikhail, Tasmin, Khadija, Ameya, Sunnah.

BVRSH - #0001 - 050722 - C26 - 229/152/8 - PB - 9781915608017 - Matt Lamination